Cambridge Elements ☰

Elements in the Economics of Emerging Markets
edited by
Bruno S. Sergi
Harvard University

COVID-19 AND ISLAMIC FINANCE

M. Kabir Hassan
University of New Orleans

Aishath Muneeza
INCEIF University

CAMBRIDGE
UNIVERSITY PRESS

CAMBRIDGE
UNIVERSITY PRESS

University Printing House, Cambridge CB2 8BS, United Kingdom

One Liberty Plaza, 20th Floor, New York, NY 10006, USA

477 Williamstown Road, Port Melbourne, VIC 3207, Australia

314–321, 3rd Floor, Plot 3, Splendor Forum, Jasola District Centre, New Delhi – 110025, India

103 Penang Road, #05–06/07, Visioncrest Commercial, Singapore 238467

Cambridge University Press is part of the University of Cambridge.

It furthers the University's mission by disseminating knowledge in the pursuit of education, learning, and research at the highest international levels of excellence.

www.cambridge.org
Information on this title: www.cambridge.org/9781009189477
DOI: 10.1017/9781009189484

First published 2022

A catalogue record for this publication is available from the British Library.

ISBN 978-1-009-18947-7 Paperback
ISSN 2631-8598 (online)
ISSN 2631-858X (print)

COVID-19 and Islamic Finance

Elements in the Economics of Emerging Markets

DOI: 10.1017/9781009189484
First published online: June 2022

M. Kabir Hassan
University of New Orleans

Aishath Muneeza
INCEIF University

Author for correspondence: M. Kabir Hassan, mhassan@uno.edu

Abstract: The objective of this Element is to provide an overview of Islamic finance by highlighting the impact of the pandemic on it in a comprehensive manner by looking at two branches of Islamic finance: Islamic commercial finance and Islamic social finance. The approach adopted in this Element is to first provide an overview of Islamic finance to the readers in a simple and easy manner followed by the impact of pandemic discussed separately for both types of Islamic finance. Last, but not least, the Element also recommends ways in which Islamic finance could be further improved in the light of the lessons learnt from the pandemic. It is anticipated that the recommendations made in this regard would assist policymakers, practitioners, researchers and other stakeholders in Islamic finance to understand the way to unlock the full potential of Islamic finance to reduce the wealth gap and achieve financial inclusion.

This Element also has a video abstract: www.cambridge.org/
hassan-muneeza
Keywords: Islamic finance, Islamic social finance, Islamic commercial finance, riba, Shariah

ISBNs: 9781009189477 (PB), 9781009189484 (OC)
ISSNs: 2631-8598 (online), 2631-858X (print)

Contents

1 Introduction: Basics of Islamic Finance

1.1 What Is Islamic Finance?

Islamic finance refers to financial activities that comply with Shariah. Shariah is known as Islamic law. The way in which Islamic finance modes are structured is that all transactions will comply with Shariah. If Shariah compliance is compromised, then there will be consequences that the Islamic financial institutions offering Islamic financial services will have to face. The consequences which the Islamic financial institutions will face in this regard include financial consequences, non-financial consequences and statutory consequences. The financial consequences that may arise due to Shariah non-compliance of Islamic financial institutions happen when the Islamic financial institutions are required to give the profits derived from Shariah-non-compliant transactions to charity to purify them. From the Shariah perspective, such profits are given to charity as an act to purify the Shariah non-compliant income received. Non-financial consequences which an Islamic financial institution may face include the reputational risk that may arise due to Shariah-non-compliant events that happen in that institution, adversely affecting the confidence of customers and other stakeholders in the financial products and services offered by Islamic financial institutions. Such reputational damages, which are non-quantifiable, can lead to substantial financial loss of Islamic financial institutions as well. In some countries like Malaysia, Shariah non-compliance of an Islamic financial institution may trigger statutory consequences where the law provides the result of Shariah non-compliance in the form of punishments like stipulating fines and/or imprisonment for the persons in charge. To adhere to Shariah principles within Islamic financial institutions, Shariah governance principles are adopted, such as having a Shariah organ within the Islamic financial institution to advise on Shariah-related matters and having internal Shariah control functions such as Shariah risk management, Shariah review and Shariah audit. Islamic financial products and services are also offered by institutions or companies other than Islamic financial institutions, such as companies offering sukuk (Islamic bonds) in Islamic capital markets. In such instances, the Shariah governance requirements applied and adopted by these institutions or companies are different from those of Islamic financial institutions. Instead of having the Shariah organs established internally and adopting internal Shariah control functions, these institutions are merely required to appoint a Shariah adviser to structure the Shariah-compliant financial instrument and adhere to what is stipulated by the appointed Shariah adviser until the maturity of the financial product. Likewise, for companies who are offering Shariah-compliant stocks, the procedure of Shariah screening is applied to find out their Shariah-compliant status.

Therefore, in a nutshell it can be stated that Islamic finance consists of those commercial transactions that are structured in accordance with Shariah, and Shariah compliance is mandatory in all Islamic finance transactions. Depending on the type of Islamic financial transaction, there are certain Shariah governance standards formulated in the world today that must be adhered to. If not, there are certain consequences that must be faced.

The institutionalization of Islamic finance in modern times began with the inception of the first Islamic bank, Mit Ghamr Savings Bank in Egypt, in 1963. Though the operation of the very first Islamic bank did not last for a long period due to political turmoil in Egypt, in 1975, Dubai Islamic Bank and Islamic Development Bank (IsDB) were established. In terms of institutionalization of takaful, the first takaful (Islamic insurance) company was incorporated in 1979 in Sudan. The first corporate sukuk was issued in 1990 by Shell MDS in Malaysia. Shariah screening of stocks to facilitate Muslim investors was introduced in 1995 by the Securities Commission of Malaysia for listed companies. In 2002, Malaysia pioneered the global sukuk market by launching the first global sukuk, and in 2005, the first Islamic real estate investment trust (i-REIT) was launched in Malaysia. It is imperative to note that Islamic finance in the world has developed gradually, and the development of it varies from one country to another depending on the political will and support given to develop it.

It is believed that the total assets of global Islamic financial services industry are at USD 2.70 trillion in 2020 (IFSB,2021). In terms of geographical presence of Islamic finance assets, it is found that 48.9 per cent of Islamic financial assets are in the Gulf Cooperation Council (GCC) region, while 24.9 per cent of them are found in the Middle East and South Asian regions; 20.3 per cent of them are found in the South-East Asia region; 1.7 per cent of them are found in the Africa region; and 4.3 per cent of them are found in other regions (IFSB, 2021). Despite the challenges faced by the pandemic, Islamic finance developments are being witnessed in the world, and the potential of Islamic finance to be the alternative financial system to conventional finance system has been realised.

1.2 Differences between Conventional and Islamic Finance

Conventional finance can be described as financial activities that are structured using money as the underlying asset to make profit. Making money out of money is the fundamental way in which conventional financial transactions operate. The typical way in which conventional financial activities are structured is using a loan transaction, where interest is stipulated to capture the time value of money. In this process, simple interest and compound interest can also be charged. From a Shariah perspective, the issue with conventional finance is that all conventional financing transactions involve riba, which is prohibited. In Shariah, a loan contract is known as qard, which is supposed to be a benevolent or a gratuitous contract which should only be used to help the parties without charging any amount extra over the principal amount given. If a loan is given, it should be given without making a profit, as it is a contract that is used in Shariah for social purposes only. In a loan transaction, if any amount is stipulated more than the principal amount given, then that extra amount, whether it is stipulated up front or later on, is known as riba al Jahiliyyah. There are two types of riba: riba al Jahiliyyah and riba al Fadl. Riba al Jahiliyyah is the riba known from the Quran that arises when simple or compound interest is charged on a loan. Riba al Fadl is known from the Sunnah (tradition of the Prophet (SAW)), where, if the ribawi commodities – gold for gold, silver for silver, barley for barley, wheat for wheat, salt for salt and dates for dates – are not exchanged on spot and in the same amount, the delay of time or extra amount exchanged will trigger riba.

To avoid the riba which is triggered in conventional financing transactions, Muslim scholars attempted to remove the element of riba by replacing the loan transaction with bai' (sale) transactions. This is because in the Quran it is explicitly stated that Allah (SW) has prohibited riba and has permitted bai'. Therefore, instead of providing loans with interest and making money out of money, in Islamic finance transactions, bai' activities are conducted to generate profit in such a manner that all parties engaging in the transaction share risk between them in a fair manner. However, there are certain fundamental Shariah rules that must be adhered to in conducting bai'. Irrespective of the type of bai' transaction, in all bai' transactions, the parties involved in the transaction must have the legal capacity to enter into the transaction and there should be no element of excessive gharar (uncertainty) involved in the transaction. The subject matter of the sale shall be in existence as well as under the ownership and possession of the seller at the time of making of the contract except in two sales: istisna' (manufacturing contract) and salam (forward sale). Further, no element of maysir (gambling) should be allowed in such a transaction, and the subject matter of the transaction must be Shariah-compliant. Apart from these general conditions of bai', there are also specific conditions that would be applied in conducting specific sale transactions.

In Islamic finance, there are various Shariah-compliant contracts used to structure the financial transactions. These include sale contracts, lease contracts, partnership contracts and service contracts. In addition to these types of contracts, there are also security contracts which are used to secure the future debt obligations. In short, it can be said that in Islamic finance transactions, the way the parties engaged in the transaction receive profit is by receiving the price of sale of an asset, by receiving the rent for a leased property, by receiving wages for a service provided, or by receiving profit by entering into a partnership to engage in a Shariah-compliant activity. This simply means that in Islamic finance transactions using money, first an underlying asset is purchased or a real economic activity is engaged to make profit. There is no situation in Islamic finance transactions where a loan is given to make profit by charging interest. However, an interest-free loan can be given. Table 1 illustrates the most common Shariah-compliant contracts used to structure Islamic finance transactions with the Shariah parameters that ought to be followed in using them.

1.3 Principles of Islamic Finance

There are certain principles of Islamic finance that need to be followed in all types of Islamic financial transactions. Apart from the principles of Islamic finance mentioned in the following sections, the prohibition against using Shariah non-compliant assets and activities and the allowing of use of Shariah-compliant commercial contracts to structure Islamic finance products and services are also some of the important principles adhered in Islamic finance.

1.3.1 Elimination of Riba

Riba literally means increase or excess. There are four stages found in the Quran for prohibition of riba. The first stage is found in Surah 30:39 of the Quran, where it is stated that riba transactions will have no blessings from Allah (SW), while the second stage is found in Surah 4:161 of the Quran, where it is stated that taking riba is equivalent to eating of wealth unlawfully. The third stage is found in Surah 3:130 of the Quran, where it is asked that believers not devour usury doubled and multiplied and to fear Allah (SW); and the final stage is found in Surah 2:275 of the Quran, where it is expressly stated that Allah (SW) has forbidden riba while stating that trading is permitted. There are two types of riba, and these types are shown in Table 2.

1.3.2 Elimination of Excessive Gharar

Gharar is uncertainty, and excessive uncertainty (Gharar Fahishah) needs to be eliminated in all Islamic finance transactions. This is the general rule applied to Islamic finance transactions. However, there are two exceptional sale contracts in Shariah, Salam and istisna' contracts, where the sale could be concluded even though the subject matter is not in existence at the time of the sale. There is no specific mention of the word gharar in the Quran; however, jurists have considered gharar with the practice of vanity (al

Table 1 Most common Shariah-compliant contracts used to structure Islamic finance transactions

Shariah-Compliant Contract	Nature	Description
Murabahah (cost plus profit sale)	Sale	Murabahah is a trust sale. Therefore, it is mandatory for the seller to disclose the acquisition price of the asset sold, and the profit charged must also be disclosed to the buyer. Further, in modern times, though classically Murabahah is a spot sale, to suit the needs of the financial institutions, it is structured as a deferred sale. Therefore, the price of the sale must be fixed at the time of sale, and the duration of the deferred sale with instalment amount for the period must be agreed upon by and clear to both parties.
Bai' Muajjal (Deferred sale)	Sale	Bai' Muajjal is a deferred sale, also known as Bai' Bithaman Ajil or Bai' bil Taqsit, where the price of the asset sold must be fixed and clear to both parties, with the period of deferred sale with instalment amount and frequency.
Tawarruq (Monetization or tripartite sale)	Sale	Tawarruq is a sale transaction where one party will sell an asset on a deferred basis to a party who needs cash; who will subsequently sell the asset sold to a third party on the spot. In this transaction, there should be three independent parties involved and the conditions of a deferred sale must be observed in the first transaction.

Table 1 (cont.)

Shariah-Compliant Contract	Nature	Description
Salam (Forward sale)	Sale (Exceptional)	Salam is a forward sale which can only be used for selling of homogeneous goods where the subject matter of sale cannot be gold or silver or precious stones. In entering into a salam contract, the quality and quantity of the goods with price must be determined at the time of concluding the contract. Also, it is mandatory to pay the price of the goods fully at the time of entering into the contract. The date of delivery must be fixed, and availability of the goods sold in the market is also a requirement.
Istisna' (Manufacturing contract)	Sale (Exceptional)	Istisna' is a manufacturing contract where the person requesting to manufacture the goods will provide specification to the manufacturer and the price will be determined at the time of the contract with the schedule of payment. Unlike in a Salam contract, in an istisna' contract, the parties have the freedom to decide the way in which they intend to pay the price. The delivery date also will be fixed. To qualify for an istisna' contract, it is the manufacturer who shall provide both the raw materials and the labour to manufacture the good.
Ijarah (Lease)	Lease	Ijarah is a leasing contract where an asset can be leased for a rent and a person can be hired to obtain a service for a wage. A perishable good cannot be leased, as the subject matter will be destroyed upon using of it. Unlike in a sale contract, in a leasing contract, the ownership of the asset leased will not

transfer from lessor to lessee; but it is the right over the usufruct of the asset that will be transferred for an agreed period of time. Upon the expiry of the lease period, the leased asset will be returned to the lessor. The lessor in this case should be the owner of the asset or should have the legal capacity or authority to lease the asset. In a lease contract, the rent amount and the lease period including the frequency of rent payment should be clear to both parties, and the operational cost related to the leased asset must be borne by the lessor. The liability for the lessee to pay rent to the asset will start only when he/she is given the asset by the lessor.

Mudharabah (Money management partnership)	Equity	Mudharabah is a money management partnership contract where one party gives capital and the other party agrees to manage the money in a Shariah-compliant business. They will agree to a pre-agreed profit sharing ratio, and no amount of profit or capital can be guaranteed. In case of loss, except in case of negligence, all the financial loss shall be borne by the capital provider, whereas the non-financial loss will be borne by the managing partner.
Musharakah (Partnership)	Equity	Musharakah is a partnership contract where the partners have the flexibility to decide what they would like to contribute to the business (capital and/or work and/or reputation). However, they have to agree to a pre-agreed profit sharing ratio, and no amount of profit or capital can be guaranteed. In case of loss, loss will depend on the capital contribution made by the parties.

Table 1 (cont.)

Shariah-Compliant Contract	Nature	Description
Wakalah (Agency)	Service	Wakalah is an agency contract where a fee can be charged for the service provided as an agent. The service of agency can also be provided for free. However, if such a service is provided for free, then it would be a non-binding contract. In this contract, the terms of the work delegated to the agent by the principal shall be clear and the agent shall follow the advice given by the principal. The agent should not go beyond the authority given by the principal and should act as a trustee in discharging his/her duties. If a fee is given, the fee must be clear to both parties and the amount of the fee can be in any manner the parties consent.

Table 2 Types of riba

Type	Explanation
Riba al Jahiliyya	Riba al Jahiliyyah is also known as riba known from the Quran. Another name for this type of riba is riba al duyun (which means the riba that arises from a loan transaction). This type of riba arises when an extra amount is stipulated in a loan contract to be paid on top of the principal payment. The upfront stipulation of any excess to the principal amount in a loan contract or stipulation of an extra amount due to delay of the principal amount will trigger this type of riba. Further, in these circumstances, this type of riba will arise even if the extra stipulated amount over the principal amount of the loan is significant or insignificant.
Riba al Fadl	Riba al Fadl is also known as riba known from Sunnah. Another name for this type of riba is riba al buyu' (which means the riba that arises from exchange of ribawi commodities, which are gold, silver, barley, wheat, dates and salt). The following hadith establish the rules of riba al Fadl: 'It was narrated that Muslim bin Yasar and 'Abdullah bin 'Atik said: "Ubadah bin As-Samit and Muawiyah met at a stopping place on the road. 'Ubadah told them: 'The Messenger of Allah forbade selling gold for gold, silver for silver, wheat for wheat, barley for barley, dates for dates' - one of them said: 'salt for salt', but the other did not say it - 'unless it was like for like, hand to hand. And he commanded us to sell gold for silver and silver for gold, and wheat for barley and barley for wheat, and to hand, however we wanted.' And one of them said: 'Whoever gives more or asks for more has engaged in Riba.'" (Sunan an-Nasa'i 4560). From the above hadith, there are two types of goods that are found based on the way they are used: gold and silver which are used as medium of exchange; and wheat, barley, dates and salt which are used as staple foods.

batil), which is found in Surah 2:188 and 4:161 of the Quran (Al-Saati, 2003). There are various hadith that prohibit excessive gharar in sale contracts, and the reason for such a prohibition is to protect both parties entering into a sale transaction from dealing with uncertainty that may cause harm and unfairness to them. For instance, it is stated in hadith that the sale of fish in the sea or of a flying bird, the sale of an unborn calf in its mother's womb and the sale of runaway slaves or animals are prohibited. If such a transaction is entered, there is no guarantee that the seller will be able to obtain the goods and fulfil his obligation under the sale contract to deliver the asset to the buyer. As such, in Islamic finance transactions, except for salam and istisna' contracts, the subject matter shall exist at the time of the sale and it must be capable of delivery. Further, the subject matter shall be owned by the seller and must be under his/her possession at the time of the sale. If the seller is not the owner, he/she must have the legal authority to conduct the sale transaction on behalf of the owner of the asset. In a sale transaction, gharar shall be avoided not only with relation to subject matter, but it shall be voided in type and/or attribute and/or quantity of the subject matter, delivery time of the asset, price, mode of payment and frequency and duration of payment in instalment sales. The effect of a sale with gharar is that existence of excessive gharar will make the contract null and void.

1.3.3 Elimination of Maysir

Maysir is gambling, and all forms of activities that are considered to be gambling are prohibited in all Islamic finance transactions. To identify a transaction as gambling, from a general perspective, there are three requirements that shall be present concurrently in a transaction: firstly, all parties involved in the transaction shall contribute financially; secondly, the party who will gain in the transaction will be determined using luck; and finally, one party gaining in that transaction will make all the other parties lose the financial amount they have contributed. If the modus operandi of a transaction is structured in such a manner, then the element of gambling will exist in it, making the transaction invalid from the Shariah perspective. Maysir is also is an excessive gharar. Surah 5:90 of the Quran explicitly prohibits engaging in maysir.

1.3.4 Elimination of Dhulm

Dhulm is injustice. In all kinds of Islamic finance transactions, anything that leads to injustice or oppression shall be avoided. This should be the case even if the parties have given consent to enter into the transaction. The aim of eliminating dhulm in Islamic finance transaction is to avoid situations where one party will take advantage of the other party in commercial transactions. However, the reality is that today it is hard to know exactly what dhulm exists in a contract entered into by the parties without the assistance of an independent party to determine that. This is because there is no objective yardstick formulated that is sufficient to be used for this purpose. As such, both parties entering into a commercial transaction should ensure that unfair terms and conditions are removed before entering into such transactions, and even after entering into the transaction, anything that will lead to oppression shall be avoided. For instance, a rich person who has a debt and intentionally delays the payment of it is causing oppression as understood from a hadith.

1.3.5 Risk Sharing Should Exist in an Equitable Manner

In Islamic finance transactions, risk sharing is promoted between the parties in an equitable and just manner. Risk can be defined as the probability of an event happening that may result in a loss. In conventional finance, the risk that results in non-payment or delay in the payment of loan or default risk is transferred to the customer or debtor by charging interest for late payment. In Islamic finance transactions, the Shariah contracts used to structure Islamic finance transactions determine the risk that each party will have to bear in the transaction. For example, in equity contracts, neither profit nor capital shall be guaranteed. A pre-agreed profit-sharing ratio must be agreed on at the time of entering into the contract, and once the profit is realised, it must be distributed accordingly. It is essential to note that risk mitigation tools and techniques can be used in Islamic finance as long as these tools and techniques do not breach the fundamental Shariah principles adopted in the Shariah contracts used to structure the respective product. The principle of "Al-ghunm bi al-ghurm" (a person is entitled to a gain if the person agrees to accept the responsibility for the loss) is promoted in Islamic finance in equity contracts.

2 Types and Components of Islamic Finance

Based on the objective of offering of Islamic finance products and services, Islamic finance can be classified into two broad categories: Islamic commercial finance and Islamic social finance. Islamic commercial finance can be defined as Islamic financial products and services offered with a view toward making profit, while Islamic social finance can be defined as Islamic financial products and services offered to benefit the society with or without making a profit. It is essential to note that Islamic social finance products can be structured in a manner such that profits can be made through the offering of such products and services and there are no issues with such practice. The important consideration in such products and services is that their first and foremost objective would be to assist the society to achieve equitable justice via financial inclusion.

There are different components of Islamic commercial finance and Islamic social finance as well. The components of Islamic commercial finance are Islamic banking, takaful and Islamic capital markets. The components of Islamic social finance include zakat, sadaqat or infaq, waqf, social takaful and Islamic microfinance. Each of these components of Islamic finance based on its classification is discussed in the following sections.

2.1 Components of Islamic Commercial Finance

2.1.1 Islamic Banking

Islamic banking is Shariah-compliant banking which adheres to Shariah principles in structuring its financial products and services. In some countries, instead of the term Islamic banking, the expression used is interest-free banking (Nigeria) or participation banking (Turkey) or participatory banking (Morocco). The fundamental difference between conventional banking and Islamic banking is that in conventional banking, the depositors, by placing their money in a current or savings or fixed deposit account, create a creditor–debtor relationship with the bank. This legal relationship has been confirmed in the landmark English case of *Foley* v. *Hill* 2 HLC 28, 9 ER 1002, where it is held that conventional banks do not hold the sums in a bank account on trust for their customers, but rather the relationship between bank and customer is that of debtor and creditor. If it is a current account which is opened, then the customer can withdraw the amount upon demand and is not entitled to get any interest for the money kept. However, if the customer keeps his money in a savings or a fixed-deposit account, then the money can only be withdrawn by the depositor as per the terms agreed with the bank, and the depositor in this case is entitled to receive profit. Using the money deposited, the conventional bank will give loans to third parties and simple and/or compound interest will be charged, considering the time value of money. From a Shariah perspective, conventional banking is prohibited for Muslims, as it is tainted with riba, which is forbidden. Therefore, in introducing Islamic banking, the main attention of Muslim scholars was to remove the Shariah-non-compliant elements from conventional banking and to make banking usable to Muslims.

It is imperative to understand the Shariah-non-compliant element found in conventional banking which is riba and how it is triggered. If a depositor keeps money in a current account at a conventional bank, then the bank as the creditor is obliged to return the exact amount kept with the bank without any interest.

Therefore, there is no Shariah-non-compliant element in dealing with current account. However, the issue in this context would arise when depositors, by keeping their money in a conventional bank, help the conventional banks to grow, which promotes riba. As such, except in cases of extreme necessity, Muslims shall not deal with conventional banks, and even if they were to deal with them, they could only open a current account. Unlike the case of the current account, if a depositor opens a saving or a fixed-deposit account and keeps money in a conventional bank, giving of interest is considered as riba due to the fact that the money deposited creates a debtor–creditor relation between the depositor and the bank, where the deposited money is viewed as a loan and any extra amount, whether significant or negligible, will be considered as riba. Likewise, when a conventional bank offers loans to third parties with interest, whether simple or compound interest, that extra amount charged over the principal is considered as riba from the Shariah perspective. Therefore, to make the banking Shariah-compliant, the debtor–creditor relationship created in conventional banking is removed by changing the nature of the relationship except in a current account, where the relationship created between the depositor and the Islamic bank would be based on qard (loan), which creates a debtor–creditor relation with no extra amount given. Since there is no extra amount given over the principal by the depositor to the Islamic bank, there is no Shariah-non-compliant element. Therefore, no change is required in this case to make it Shariah-compliant.

To open a saving account or an account equivalent to a fixed-deposit account of a conventional bank, a profit-sharing contract known as Mudharabah is created. Mudharabah is a Shariah-compliant equity contract where one party provides capital and the other party manages the capital by investing it in a Shariah-compliant business activity. The parties in this case will have to determine a pre-agreed profit-sharing ratio, and in case of loss, except in case of negligence, all financial loss will be borne by the capital provider. Non-financial losses will be borne by the manager. In a Mudharabah contract no amount of capital nor profit shall be guaranteed. Therefore, if the concept of Mudharabah is used to structure a bank account equivalent to the fixed-deposit account of a conventional bank, then the name of the account will change to investment account. In a saving or investment account of an Islamic bank structured using Mudharabah, the capital provider would be the depositor, and the Islamic bank the manager. To give a fixed return to the depositors like in the case of conventional banks, Islamic banks can structure their saving or investment accounts using the Shariah concept of tawarruq (tripartite sale) or commodity Murabahah (cost plus profit sale). The modus operandi of this type of deposit product would be as follows: first, a specific asset will be identified and used as an underlying asset for the sale and purchase transactions between the Islamic bank and the customer where the customer will authorise the Islamic Bank to enter into a transaction on the customer's behalf based on the agreed terms and conditions. Subsequently, the Islamic bank as the agent of the customer will purchase the commodity from a broker for spot value. The Islamic bank will then offer to the customer to buy the commodity at cost plus profit which is to be paid on the specific deferred payment date. The Islamic bank will then sell the commodity to another broker for settlement spot value. Upon the deferred payment date, the Islamic bank will pay the customer the sale price amount, which consists of cost (principal) plus profit. What is important to understand here is that Shariah-compliant trade contracts are used to ensure that profits made by Islamic banks or customers through Islamic banks are halal (permissible). The same concept is used by Islamic banks to provide financing to third parties as well. Instead of providing loans, Islamic banks engage in trading activities such as selling of an asset or leasing of an asset or providing of a permissible service or entering into a partnership contract to generate halal profit while providing financing to those who need it. Therefore, Islamic banks do not use the term 'loan', instead calling it 'financing facilities'. An example to illustrate how a facility for property financing can be offered by Islamic banks using a Musharakah Mutanaqisa (diminishing partnership) is where the customer and the Islamic bank jointly acquire and own a property. The Islamic bank will then lease the property to the customer, and the instalment payments shall gradually transfer the Islamic bank's ownership to the customer. Further, like conventional banks, Islamic banks also take collateral to ensure that the receivables arising from the sale or lease or partnership-based contracts are duly received. Unlike conventional banks, Islamic banks do not charge compound interest for late payment; but ta'waidh (fixed amount paid as compensation for actual loss considered as the bank's income) and gharamah (penalty interest which is given to charity) can be charged by following the Shariah requirements.

It is essential to note that Islamic banking services are not only provided by full-fledged Islamic banks. Some countries allow conventional banks to operate 'Islamic windows' to provide Islamic banking services by ensuring that conventional and Islamic funds are not co-mingled by adhering to proper Shariah governance rules. Conventional banks can offer Islamic financial services in this manner only if the respective regulatory authority of the country allows it. For instance, in 2011 Qatar banned Islamic window operation in onshore conventional banks and in 2012 extended the Islamic window ban (Reuters, 2012). The general idea of having such window operations is to pave the way for development of Islamic finance services within conventional banks until they are fully ready to offer such services by incorporating a subsidiary (Solé, 2017).

For instance, in Indonesia, Regulation No.11/10/PBI/2009 requires conventional banks to spin off Islamic windows when the assets of the Islamic window reach 50 per cent of those of its parent. The regulation also requires conventional banks to establish separate Islamic business units by 2023 or 15 years after the enactments of Law No. 21 of 2008 on Islamic banking (Hasan and Risfandy, 2021).

2.1.2 Takaful

Takaful is Islamic insurance, and it is structured using Shariah-compliant concepts and contracts. The main reason for the need to introduce takaful was the Shariah non-compliance issue detected in the way conventional insurance is practiced. Conventional insurance is a sale contract where the insurance company sells an insurance policy to the policyholder for a consideration which is for the payment of the premium as agreed. The subject matter of this sales transaction is the insurance policy in which it is stated that the benefit from it will be given to the policyholder upon happening of the unfortunate events described which are covered in the policy and which do not fall within the excluded events stated in it. The Shariah issue triggered here is that in sales contracts, certain elements must be present, and there should be no element of excessive uncertainty on the subject matter of the sale. Not only this, but it is essential in a sales contract for the subject matter of it to be transferred from the seller to the buyer upon conclusion of the contract. But in the case of conventional insurance, it is unclear what is the subject matter of the sale of which the ownership has been transferred from the seller to the buyer. Therefore, from the Shariah perspective, a conventional insurance contract cannot be considered to be a sale contract. As such, to ensure that conventional insurance is changed to a Shariah-compliant transaction, Muslim scholars changed the sale contract to a tabarru' (charity) contract. Islam encourages Muslims to help each other in doing and promoting good, while forbidding what is evil. As such, with this intention Shariah permits individuals in the society to provide guarantees to assist each other in overcoming unfortunate circumstances that may occur unexpectedly. The word takaful is derived from the word 'Kafalah' which means a guarantee where the principle of joint cooperation (ta'aawun) between each individual is promoted. In Islamic commercial takaful, different models are adopted to facilitate the takaful operator or the provider to earn a halal (lawful) income. Certain governance rules are followed as well in managing the contributions received from the takaful participants. In takaful arrangements, the name given to the insurance company is that of the takaful operator, while the policyholders are called participants or contributors and the premium paid is known as contributions made. Two distinctive funds are handled by the takaful operators: shareholder's fund and contributor's fund. The undertakings given for charity received from the contributors will be managed in the contributor's fund, and this fund does not belong to the takaful operator. One of the prevalent takaful operation models adopted in the world is based on the Shariah concept of 'wakalah' (agency contract). In this model, the contributors appoint the takaful operator as their wakeel (agent) to manage their contributions, and as a consideration to that, the wakeel is paid a fixed commission or a fee. As such, in this type of takaful model, the fixed commission will be deducted from the contribution paid by the takaful participants, and it is the fixed commission that will go to the shareholder's fund while the balance will go to the contributor's fund. However, if a Mudharabah (money management partnership) model is adopted to provide takaful products by the takaful operator, then the takaful operator will not receive a fixed fee or a commission; they only agree to receive profit based on the pre-agreed profit-sharing ratio. If there is no profit, then they are not entitled to receive anything.

Further, the premium paid by all policyholders will be managed by the insurance company by investing it in financial instruments which are not necessarily Shariah-compliant. As such, the returns received from these investments could be tainted with riba. For instance, if part of these investments is invested in conventional treasury instruments, then the return will be tainted with interest, as this transaction is based on a loan contract where the issuer promises to give back the principal with interest after the maturity period. The same will happen even if part of it is invested in conventional bonds. Likewise, if it is invested in an equity financial product and the Shariah screening of that product is not carried out, the dividend received might be tainted with income received from Shariah-non-compliant activities. Therefore, in takaful, the takaful operator can invest only in Shariah-compliant financial instruments such as Islamic treasury instruments or Islamic bonds or Shariah-screened equities and, therefore, the return received from them is Shariah-compliant.

Lastly, at the end of the year, if there is any surplus after paying the policy-holders who claimed the money, the surplus will belong to the insurance company. Regarding this surplus, the Shariah issue detected by Muslim scholars is that this is similar to maysir (gambling). This is because, financially, all policyholders contribute as per the insurance policy they take, and it is luck that determines whether they will be able to get any benefit; and if the policyholders did not claim, it is a financial gain to the insurance company. As such, in takaful operations, the surplus in the contributor's fund will be distributed between them in the manner agreed upon, and the surplus will never automatically become the property of the takaful operator.

Takaful business can be divided into two categories: by management of takaful structure and by type of business. By looking at the management of takaful structure, it could be further categorised into mutual or cooperative takaful structure and commercial (tijari) takaful. Mutual or cooperative takaful structure is where there is no separate entity to manage the takaful contributions; rather, the contributors or participants themselves undertake the management of the takaful scheme. On the other hand, in commercial takaful, a separate legal entity is incorporated to manage the takaful scheme, and it is known as the takaful operator. By type of business, takaful can be divided into general takaful, where the focus is on short-term protection of properties and liabilities arising from any damage or loss; and family takaful, where there is a combination of long-term savings and protection for participants and their dependants which arises from death, disability, or survival.

2.1.3 Islamic Capital Markets

Islamic capital markets refer to capital market activities that are conducted in accordance with Shariah. As in conventional capital markets, in Islamic capital markets there are two distinctive markets: the equity market and the debt market. In the Islamic equity market, there are various types of equity products such as Shariah-compliant shares, Islamic unit trust, Islamic real estate investment fund, Islamic exchange traded fund, Islamic venture capital and private equity, Islamic crowdfunding and crypto assets. In the Islamic debt market, different kinds of sukuk (Islamic bonds) are available.

From the Shariah perspective, there is no issue in entering into equity relationship with each other as long as the investment is Shariah-compliant. This is because, when one invests his or her money to conduct a Shariah-non-compliant activity, then the dividend received from such activities would be considered as Shariah-non-compliant. As such, it is imperative for any Muslim investor to check whether the activities conducted by the company in which they intend to invest are Shariah-compliant or not before they invest. The process to determine the Shariah-compliant status of a company is known as the Shariah screening process. Shariah screening processes of companies were first developed in Malaysia in the 1990s with the intention of providing Muslim investors with the opportunity to invest in shares of public companies. Today, not only have regulatory authorities such as Securities Commission Malaysia formulated Shariah screening methodologies, but private companies like the Dow Jones Islamic Market Index (DJIM), launched in 1999 in Bahrain, have formulated their own methodologies.

Generally, the Shariah stock screening process involves two stages: business screening and financial screening. In the business screening stage, the primary activities of the company are screened to find out whether they engage in any of the activities prohibited in the Shariah screening criteria. If the primary activity of the company screened is any of the Shariah-non-compliant activities, then the company would be disqualified and would not be allowed to proceed with the rest of the screening stages. In this stage, further secondary activities of the company will also be checked, and the tolerance benchmark used is 5 per cent of the total asset in this regard. The next step is financial screening, where certain financial filters are used to determine different dimensions of Shariah compliance, such as the amount of cash kept in conventional banks and the amount of conventional loans obtained by the company. Certain tolerance benchmarks are formulated for this purpose, and the most common threshold used in this regard is 33 per cent. The Securities Commission Malaysia, unlike other screening bodies, employs a qualitative screening criterion like looking at the image and public interest of a company to further determine the eligibility of the company to be considered as a Shariah-compliant equity. Once the Shariah screening is completed, the tainted income or the Shariah-non-compliant part of the dividend received needs to be purified. In the case of the Shariah screening criteria formulated by the Capital Market Development Authority of Maldives, it is not the investor who is required to purify the dividend; rather, the company that applies for Shariah screening should give all its tainted income to charity. It is imperative to note that Shariah screening is not a one-off exercise, but rather is carried out as a continuous activity, the frequency of which is determined by the authority or the company conducting it. For instance, in the case of Securities Commission Malaysia, the Shariah screening of companies is conducted twice a year and the result is published. If at any point the status of a company changes from Shariah-compliant to Shariah-non-compliant, then as soon as possible the shareholder should dispose of the shares by selling them. Though this is the general norm, some rules in this regard are laid down by Shariah advisory bodies such as the statutory Shariah Advisory Council of Securities Commission Malaysia (Securities Commission Malaysia, 2020; pp. 135–136).

As for the Islamic debt market, sukuk is the alternative for a conventional bond. The Shariah issue with the conventional bond transaction is that the issuer issues the bond and promises to pay interest as agreed within the maturity period. Since this transaction is based on a loan contract, any amount given by the issuer to the bondholder over the principal amount is considered as riba. As such, sukuk transactions are designed using Islamic commercial contracts where there is an underlying asset or a real economic activity to generate profit, rather than making money out of money. The most comprehensive definition for sukuk is provided by Accounting and Auditing Organisation for Islamic Financial Institutions (AAOIFI), which states that sukuk are certificates of equal value representing undivided shares in ownership of tangible assets, usufruct and services or (in ownership of) assets of particular projects or special investment activity. Even a company which does not pass Shariah screening can issue sukuk as long as the purpose of issuing the sukuk is Shariah-compliant. There are two types of sukuk: asset-backed sukuk and asset-based sukuk. Asset-backed sukuk are those sukuk where the originator (an entity, whether a company or a government, that requires financing) transfers legal ownership of the underlying assets to a Special Purpose Vehicle (SPV), and the SPV issues the sukuk to the sukukholders. In this type of sukuk, though there will be limited recourse for sukukholders to claim for the underlying assets, the sukukholders in case of default will have the assets to recover the money owed instead of relying on the cashflow of the originator. On the other hand, in asset-based sukuk, such as conventional bonds, the sukukholders will have to rely on the cashflow of the obligor to realise the payments owed to them under the sukuk and they will have no recourse to an asset. This is because in this kind of sukuk, due to sale of an asset to the obligor by the sukukholders on a deferred basis, the sukukholders will be entitled to receive the price of the asset within the maturity period. In case of default, the receivables should be claimed by the sukukholders from the obligor and there will be no underlying asset in this kind of sukuk. Short-term sukuk are used in Islamic money markets, and the duration of these instruments is less than a year.

2.2 Components of Islamic Social Finance

2.2.1 Zakat

Zakat is the third pillar of Islam, and as such, it is considered as a worship and a commercial matter that falls within the ambit of Islamic social finance. Unlike other Islamic social finance products or institutions or instruments, zakat is a compulsory obligation for all Muslims who are eligible to pay it and the money received as zakat shall only be spent or disbursed to those who are the legal recipients of it. There are two types of zakat: zakat al fitr and zakat al maal. The conditions and the recipients of these two types of zakat differ, and as such, it is imperative to understand the differences between them. Further, it is imperative to note that any amount which is paid in excess of the amount that needed to be paid as zakat will be considered as sadaqat (charity). Therefore, often the institutions or authorities collecting zakat will also be collecting sadaqat, and in terms of disbursing sadaqat, there is much flexibility available for them, as there are no strict legal recipients of it that ought to be adhered such as in the case of zakat. Zakat literally means to grow and increase and as such, by giving zakat, the blessing of Allah (SW) on one's wealth will increase.

Zakat al fitr is the zakat that needs to be paid during the month of Ramadhan, which is the ninth month of the Muslim calendar as well as the month of fasting. The period to pay zakat al fitr starts from the beginning of Ramadhan at any time before the month ends, with the latest time being before the Eid prayer. The recipients of this type of zakat are Muslims who are poor and needy. It is obligatory for every Muslim, whether male or female, slave or freeman, or minor or major, as long as they are capable (have food in excess of their needs). The amount of zakat al fitr that needs to be paid does not depend on the income earned. The minimum amount to be paid as zakat al fitr is one saa` (four double handfuls) of food, grain or dried fruit for each person, and the household head can pay zakat al fitr for the whole family. Today, instead of paying this type of zakat in kind, even the payment of the cash equivalent amount is permitted. The main purpose of zakat al fitr is to allow all members of the society to enjoy Eid after the month of fasting through redistribution of wealth. As such, zakat al fitr shall be distributed to its recipients before the Eid prayer. It is estimated that Muslims around the world in every Ramadan distribute at least USD 15 billion as zakat al fitr (Abdullah, 2018).

Zakat al maal (wealth) payment amount depends on the amount of wealth accumulated by a person. The recipients of zakat are stated in Quran 9:60, and they are fuqara (the poor), masakin (the needy), 'amil (the zakah manager), mualafah qulobuhm (reconciled hearts), fi al-riqab (liberating slaves), al-gharimin (persons under debt), fi sabil lil Allah (for the sake of Allah) and ibn al-sabil (the wayfarer). The word zakat is mentioned thirty times in the Quran, and twenty-seven times it is mentioned after the mention of prayer, indicating this significance of zakat. Only eligible Muslims will have to pay zakat from their wealth and assets once it reaches nisab (minimum assigned on annual basis on wealth or once harvested on agriculture products). It is also a condition to pay zakat from the lawfully acquired wealth and assets. There are more than fourteen types of wealth from which zakat al maal is required to be paid. These types include zakat on livestock (animal products and fishing), zakat on rikaz (treasures buried in the earth) and minerals (gold, silver and mining), zakat on money and business (commercial, rented buildings, fixed capital jewellery, salaries, wages, bonuses, grants, gifts and dividends), and zakat on assets, grains and fruits (agriculture products, plants, agriculture lands and honey). It is estimated in a study by the World Bank and the Islamic Research and Training Institute (IRTI) of the Islamic Development Bank (IsDB) that the global zakat funds reached USD 550 billion to USD 600 billion per year, and it is only USD 10 billion to

USD 15 billion per year which the official zakat institutions are able to manage (Widadio, 2019).

To enhance the administration of zakat in countries, it is imperative to enact a specific and customised legal framework which is not so rigid. For instance, it is observed that in Libya, due to rigidity in the zakat framework of the country, every year a surplus is recorded in the zakat fund (Islamic Research and Training Institute, Islamic Development Bank, 2020). This is because the zakat legal framework of Libya stipulates the rate of zakat distribution for each category that cannot be violated (Islamic Research and Training Institute, Islamic Development Bank, 2020). To have an efficient zakat fund, a high level of community awareness about the significance of zakat is required and human capital development needs to be focused (Islamic Research and Training Institute, Islamic Development Bank, 2020).

2.2.2 Sadaqat or Infaq

Sadaqat is the voluntary charity that is paid for anyone who deserves charity with the view of seeking the pleasure of Allah (SW). Infaq is also a word used to denote sadaqat. Unlike zakat, for sadaqat any amount can be paid by any person to be given to any recipient he or she desires at any time of the year. The only requirement is to have the intention to donate to seek pleasure from Allah (SW). The person who wants to donate can do it by directly giving the donation to a recipient or by giving the donation to an organisation managing them. In terms of what can be donated, it could be cash or in kind. Not only this, but one can also do charitable acts by providing a service for free like volunteering to do good. To ensure that people are encouraged to do more charity, the impact created by using charity needs to be displayed publicly. It is imperative to note that an act of a person could also be a sadaqat. For example, volunteering to do a good action or even smiling at a person can be considered a form of sadaqat. This means that giving money is not the only form of giving sadaqat; rather, one's actions also can be a way of giving sadaqat. Sadaqat is also an important Islamic social finance tool for redistribution of wealth, and it could be an important source of funding for microfinance institutions as well as those in society who need a helping hand to survive without expectation of a return. Since there is no return expected for what is spent as sadaqat, such assistance could be used to help the poor and needy to change their situation by motivating them to become financially self-sufficient. The motivation of giving sadaqat from a Shariah perspective is to earn rewards from Allah (SW) in the quest to achieve paradise. It is imperative to note that sadaqat jariya is the most reward-ing type of sadaqat which can be described as recurrent or perpetual sadaqat that will be rewarded even after the donor dies. Abdullah bin Abu Qatadah narrated that his father said, 'The Messenger of Allah said: "The best things that a man can leave behind are three: A righteous son who will pray for him, ongoing charity whose reward will reach him, and knowledge which is acted upon after his death"' (Sunan Ibn Majah, n.d.; Hadith no. 241). A typical example of a sadaqat jariya is waqf, which is explained in the next section. The acts that benefit a person even after his/her death are mentioned in a hadith of the Prophet (SAW). It was narrated that Abu Hurairah said,

> The Messenger of Allah said: 'The rewards of the good deeds that will reach a believer after his death are: Knowledge which he taught and spread; a righteous son whom he leaves behind; a copy of the Quran that he leaves as a legacy; a mosque that he built; a house that he built for wayfarers; a canal that he dug; or charity that he gave during his lifetime when he was in good health. These deeds will reach him after his death'
> (Sunan Ibn Majah, n.d.; Hadith no. 242).

2.2.3 Waqf

Waqf can be described as the Islamic endowment, and in Arabic it means to stop or withhold. A precise way to define waqf could be to state that it is a form of financial gratuitous institution incorporated by putting immovable and/or movable properties under it, which should be held in perpetuity, where the properties or the revenues received from them shall be used only for public purposes in accordance with the conditions stipulated by its founder. In short, it can be said that waqf is the appropriation of the 'ayn (property) from private ownership with the intention of dedicating its usufruct to charitable purposes in perpetuity. Waqf is considered as a continuous or recurrent act of charity or sadaqat of which the benefit or reward of such an act will continue even after the demise of its founder. Due to the perpetual effect of waqf, once a property is given as waqf, such property can never be bequeathed as a gift or inherited or disposed of by selling it. As long as the waqf property is in existence, it would remain as a property dedicated to public purposes for seeking the pleasure of Allah (SW). Since the property dedicated to waqf belongs to Allah (SW), the property will belong to Him only and it is the revenue generated from such property which will be disbursed to specific needs. Therefore, the fundamental attributes of a waqf are that once it is created, it becomes perpetual, irrevocable and inalienable. Depending on the type of property dedicated as waqf, it can be divided into waqf ghair manqul (immovable waqf) and waqf manqul (moveable waqf). Immovable waqf include immovable properties such as land, fields, farms, or buildings such as mosques, schools and hospitals, orphanages and agricultural lands, and movable waqf includes movable properties such as animals, books, crops, weapons, medical instruments, jewellery and money. The benefit of waqf includes resolving the issue of undersupply of public goods (Çizakça, 1998). To develop waqf in a sustainable manner, it is imperative to enact comprehensive legal frameworks for waqf, and a national policy on waqf needs to be enacted in countries with the objective of creating synergy between various segments of the economy (Islamic Research and Training Institute, Islamic Development Bank, 2020). Further, there is a need to recreate awareness about the importance of waqf as an Islamic socio-finance institution.

2.2.4 Social Takaful

Social takaful can be described as protection provided to the financially excluded or marginalised. On the other hand, micro-takaful is the takaful scheme for a low-income population where the service could be obtained by contributing an affordable amount. In social takaful schemes, the contribution that needs to be paid for the beneficiaries is paid by a third party, which could be the government or a company. There is limited data available on the practice of social takaful schemes, and one reason for this could be limited practice of this type of takaful in the world. In practice, it is found that social takaful is performed through social insurance schemes offered by governments which can be described as a public insurance programme that protects the vulnerable population of the country against certain economic risks such as loss of income due to old age, disability, or sickness. Even though the term takaful is not mentioned in such schemes, the modus operandi of these schemes could comply with Shariah. So far, the word takaful is being used in the social takaful schemes provided in two countries: the mySalam takaful scheme of Malaysia; and 'Takaful and Karma', a cash assistance programme, conducted in Egypt, which is a national, focussed social safety network programme with the objective of protecting the poor via income support. The objective of a social takaful scheme is to provide to the members of society protection when an unfortunate event happens. Those who are financially able and capable have the option to subscribe to commercial takaful and obtain protection for such events. However, in the case of the poor and needy or those who are financially vulnerable and unable to subscribe to such commercial takaful schemes on their own, it is the responsibility of the society or the government to assist them by providing them the protection required. Therefore, social takaful is considered an important Islamic social finance tool to assist those who are financially incapable of protecting themselves against any sudden unfortunate incidents happening in the future.

2.2.5 Islamic Microfinance

Islamic microfinance is the mechanism through which the financially excluded population is provided with financing opportunities in an affordable manner. The main difference between an Islamic microfinance institution and an Islamic bank is that the objective of Islamic microfinance institutions would be to financially empower those who are unable to access the commercial Islamic banks by providing them affordable financing, while the objective of Islamic banks would be to make maximum profit for the shareholders and the investment accountholders, including other depositors by providing financial products and services that will give maximum return to the bank. Achieving the social goals of financial inclusion is not part of the Islamic banks' formal mandate. However, there are exceptions to this general rule, as there are Islamic banks that offer microfinance under one roof also. For instance, in Bangladesh, Islami Bank Bangladesh Limited provides Islamic banking solutions that are not only for commercial purposes but also for social purposes, where small and medium enterprises (SMEs) have been provided with suitable financial products which they can afford. Rural Development Scheme, offered by Islami Bank Bangladesh Limited, is an exemplary scheme where farmers are assisted financially in managing farming and in their investment needs with the objective of alleviating poverty. In this scheme, it is found that 92 per cent of the customers involved are women (Islami Bank Bangladesh Limited, n.d.).

3 Impact of COVID-19 on Islamic Finance

3.1 Impact of COVID-19 on Islamic Commercial Finance

Despite the challenges posed by the pandemic, the global Islamic Financial Services Industry (IFSI) in 2020 saw progress, as it was projected to be worth USD 2.70 trillion in 2020 (IFSB, 2021). It is found that due to the pandemic, the takaful contributions declined slightly, while growth has been evident in the Islamic banking and Islamic capital market sector (IFSB, 2021). This section discusses the impact of the pandemic on Islamic commercial finance.

3.1.1 Islamic Banking

Islamic banking faced several challenges in the pandemic. The deposits placed at the banks were withdrawn to manage households and corporations due to loss of income/revenue, and those who took financing facilities, whether individuals or corporations, are unable to pay back their debts as agreed. Therefore, Islamic banks have faced liquidity challenges (Islamic Development Bank, 2020B). To facilitate them, some of the central banks intervened, and the Islamic banks in those jurisdictions had to provide debt moratoriums for those customers affected. This caused Islamic banks to slightly decline in their profits, as there was a decrease in the number of customers who could pay back the amount they owed to the bank as agreed (Almonifi et al., 2021), and to find innovative mechanisms to ensure that they can make profit. Islamic Financial Services Board (2020A) states that Islamic financial institutions, including Islamic banks, are better capitalised as well as more profitable and liquid in the financial crisis caused by the pandemic than they were in the global financial crisis. One of the most critical challenges some Islamic banks faced was to use technology to provide banking products and services in a socially distant manner. An enabling infrastructure, including a cybersecurity legal framework with regulatory guidance, is required for this. It is found that the most common type of technology used by Islamic banks is mobile technology/digital wallets, an artificial programming interface and biometric authentication (Islamic Financial Services Board, 2020B). In Malaysia, it is reported that due to the pandemic, in one year up to June 2021, the country saw an 89 per cent increase in volume of e-wallet transactions with 468 million transactions; participation of merchants for QR code payments increased 57 per cent with one million registrations; and online banking transaction volume increased 36 per cent with 12.1 billion transactions (Abdul Aziz, 2021). Likewise, a mechanism to assist customers who are unable to pay their debt despite being granted a debt moratorium was also an issue that required a sustainable solution. Further, Islamic banks have also strengthened corporate social responsibility (CSR) initiatives. In this regard, for instance, the first full-fledged Islamic bank in Malaysia, Bank Islam Malaysia Bhd, has reported that as of 31 December 2020, the bank has spent about RM 2.2 million for CSR initiatives with 5,800 volunteer hours, which benefited more than 4,500 members of the society (Bank Islam Malaysia Bhd, 2020). Likewise, even Islamic social finance tools were also used by Islamic banks to assist the needy in the midst of the pandemic. For instance, it is reported that Bank Islam Malaysia Bhd had used sadaqat, waqf and zakat to support the needy, where it is reported that through the Islamic crowdfunding platform Sadaqah House, RM 400,000 was raised to assist those in Johore and Pahang affected by floods while they were struggling to survive under the hardships caused by the pandemic (Bank Islam Malaysia Bhd, 2020). Following are some case studies to show the role of Islamic banks in the midst of the pandemic in adapting to the unprecedented event.

Case Study 1: Dubai Islamic Bank, UAE

Dubai Islamic Bank in the midst of the pandemic has offered digital-based solutions to its customers where online and mobile banking services have been improvised to suit the needs of the customers. It is said that personal finance and credit cards could be obtained within a few minutes using these digital channels. The bank promotes cashless payment modes. The bank also provides relief to those eligible under the Targeted Economic Support Scheme (TESS) announced by the Central Bank (CB) of the UAE on 18 March 2020 to provide temporary relief for all affected private sector corporations, SMEs and individuals, which was effective only from 15 March 2020 until 30 June 2021. This scheme is applicable to financial products, and the eligible customers can request the postponement of financial payments. It is revealed that the total income of the bank reached AED 13,142 million in the year 2020 where the figure in 2019 was AED 13,684 million, showing only a marginal decline (Dubai Islamic Bank, 2021). The operating revenue of the bank increased to AED 9,471 million; group net profit declined by 38 per cent to AED 3,160 million; and the bank continued to give support to customers impacted by the COVID-19 pandemic during 2020 by providing relief measures of nearly AED 9 billion to over 54,000 retail and corporate customers of the bank.

Case Study 2: Financial Management and Resilience Programme (Urus) to Assist "Bottom 50" Customers of Banks in Malaysia

In Malaysia, it is reported that the banks, including Islamic banks via Association of Banks in Malaysia, Association of Islamic Banking and Financial Institutions Malaysia and Association of Development Finance Institutions of Malaysia, have collaborated with the Credit Counselling and Management Agency (AKPK) by introducing the Financial Management and Resilience Programme (Urus). The objective of Urus is to assist B50 customers who are having difficulty in paying their financing facilities due to financial hardship caused to them by the pandemic (The Sun Daily, 2021). Urus has allocated RM 1 billion to fund the cost of reduction in profit costs, including a profit waiver made for B50 customers to recover from financial hardship (The Sun Daily, 2021). The customers eligible to apply this scheme are those individuals who are under an existing repayment assistance program as of 30 September 2021 and are in a B50 segment of population whose gross household income is RM 5,880 or less; who have experienced 50 per cent reduction of income or loss of employment; and whose financing facility is still a performing financing facility (not in arrears exceeding 90 days) at the time of application (The Sun Daily, 2021). Under Urus, the customers will be provided with a personalised or customised financial plan by AKPK to ensure that the respective customers could enjoy financial relief. The financial plan will give the liberty for customers to choose one of the following two options: a profit waiver for three months from the date of the month following the customer's onboarding into the scheme; or a three-month profit waiver together with reduced instalments for a period of up to 24 months in total (The Sun Daily, 2021). Customers with unsecured personal loans/financing and credit cards during this period may also enjoy reduced profit rates to ease their financial hardship (The Sun Daily, 2021).

3.1.2 Takaful

Like other components of Islamic commercial finance, even takaful industry has been adversely affected due to the pandemic. However, it is found that the takaful contributions declined only slightly due to the pandemic (IFSB, 2021). As the incomes of corporations and individuals have been affected, for the existing takaful policies, the contributions that ought to be paid declined, causing the policies to lapse, and it became hard for takaful companies to get new business. In some countries like Malaysia, the Central Bank also made takaful companies provide debt moratoriums to takaful contributions as well if the contributors are adversely affected due to pandemic (Bank Negara Malaysia, 2021). Therefore, the revenue of the takaful companies also declined due to the pandemic, and as governments stepped in to provide free healthcare for COVID-infected patients, some takaful companies have experienced considerable surplus in the medical takaful sector due to this, while motor vehicle takaful is another sector. On the other hand, due to fall in new car sales, decline in takaful contributions made for motor vehicles was evident (Augustine, 2021). For instance, it is reported that Saudi Arabia is the country in GCC which contributes to 85 per cent of total gross written premiums of all takaful providers in the region, and in 2020, a 2.9 per cent decline of motor business was seen, while a decline of 6.8 per cent was evident in the first quarter of 2021 (Augustine, 2021). To ensure that the takaful companies could be relevant to the situation and cater to the demand of customers, new innovative takaful solutions such as introducing takaful coverages for side effects of COVID-19 vaccines are being introduced (Malaysian Takaful Association, 2021). Further, in some countries like Malaysia, a COVID-19 test fund has been launched to subsidise the cost of the contributors in takaful and policyholders in insurance who are most at risk for COVID-19, with a maximum reimbursement of RM 300 per test which is limited to one reimbursement per individual (Insurance Services Malaysia Bhd, 2021). According to IFSB (2021), for the takaful sector not much data was available, and it was found that neither significant decline nor significant increase in contributions was seen in the takaful sector. The health takaful category was not affected adversely much, while motor claims have declined due to lockdown (IFSB, 2021). Following are some case studies to show how takaful companies have adapted to the pandemic.

Case Study 1: AIA PUBLIC Takaful Bhd.

AIA PUBLIC Takaful Bhd. is jointly owned by AIA Bhd. (AIA) and Public Bank Berhad (PBB), and Public Islamic Bank Berhad (a wholly owned subsidiary of PBB) is a takaful company incorporated on 11 March 2011 in Malaysia. AIA PUBLIC Takaful Bhd. introduced medical plans covering the hospital treatment charges for COVID-19; and all AIA medical plans cover the policy/certificate holders' medical treatments for any complications or side effects that he/she may experience which require hospital admission after taking the approved COVID-19 vaccine (Malaysian Takaful Association, 2021). Under the COVID-19 relief program, the eligible certificate holders can apply to temporarily defer paying their regular contribution while their family takaful protection coverage continues. Certificate holders can delay their premium contribution for three consecutive months if their application for this deferment is approved by AIA. However, since this is not a waiver of the contribution program, the certificate holder will have to pay back the outstanding contribution(s) once the deferment has ended to make sure that the policy/certificate remains active and its sustainability is not impacted. This deferment option is applicable only to Individual Family Takaful certificates by AIA PUBLIC Takaful Bhd. On 8 June 2021, it was announced that Malaysians and their families would be offered COVID-19 Vaccine Complications Cover and COVID-19 Diagnosis Cover at no additional cost (AIA PUBLIC Takaful Bhd, 2021).

Case Study 2: Takaful Brunei Keluarga

Takaful Brunei Keluarga (TBK) is a takaful provider in Brunei who has been providing takaful services for over twenty years. For new and existing takaful contributors of its protection and savings plans, TBK is providing free COVID-19 special coverage (The Scoop, 2021). If any of the contributors is hospitalised due to COVID-19 virus infection, a cash payout of Brunei Dollar 1,500 will be given and participants also may opt to top up their monthly contribution of Brunei Dollar 13.20 to have an added hospital cash benefit of up to Brunei Dollar 200 daily within the validity period (The Scoop, 2021). The savings plans to which coverage against COVID-19 is given are Nur Savings Takaful, Education Takaful, Saving Takaful, Retirement Takaful, Hajj/Umrah Takaful, Dream House Takaful, Walimatul Urus Takaful and Tarbiyah Takaful (The Scoop, 2021). Not only this, but under the corporate social responsibility of the company, it has assisted poor and needy in the community even in the midst of the pandemic. For instance, in September 2020, it was reported that to prevent the spread of the virus and to assist students and teachers, TBK donated 33 bottles of 500 ml ethanol disinfectants to Raja Isteri Girls High School (STRPI) (Takaful Brunei, 2020).

3.1.3 Islamic Capital Market

Equity Market

There are numerous studies published on the impact of the pandemic on Islamic equity markets where comparison is made with the conventional equity market. For instance, Nomran and Haron (2021) conducted an empirical study to find out the impact of the pandemic on stock market return of both conventional and Islamic stocks. The findings of this study revealed that Islamic stocks performed much better than conventional stocks before and even during the pandemic. Therefore, it was believed that Islamic stock markets offer a better hedge against the pandemic compared to conventional stock markets. Similar results are shown in studies conducted by Ashraf et al., (2020) and Ahmed (2020), where it was indicated that during the pandemic Islamic stocks outperformed conventional stocks. However, an empirical study has been conducted by Arif et al. (2021) where a comparison between the pandemic and the global financial crisis was made to find out whether Islamic stocks can be considered as a safe haven for Group of Seven (G7) stock markets. The findings of this study revealed that Islamic indices do not possess safe-haven properties for the G7 group index and any of the G7 country indices. The study conducted by Yarovaya et al. (2020) shows that due to the spillover effects from conventional to Islamic stock index, Islamic stock index becomes much stronger in the pandemic. In a country-specific study, it was found that Islamic stock markets in Turkey are more stable and resilient than conventional stock markets during the pandemic (Erdoğan et al., 2020). It is also imperative to note that the impact of the pandemic on Islamic stock markets may differ from sector to sector. For instance, it was found that in the UK, stock returns in the information technology sector performed better during the pandemic than those in consumer discretionary sectors such as leisure, tourism, transportation and beverages (Sherif, 2020).

In the beginning of the year 2020, a bull market was seen, followed by a short bear market, and again followed by a bull market. The volatility seen in the Islamic equity market is due to the shock created by the pandemic which was recovered later on due to fiscal and monetary support from governments and the successful trial of vaccines which led to opening of sectors in the economy. It is reported that the technological sector in the Islamic equity market outperformed the other sectors, and this is due to the complete shift of physical human interactions to online human interactions for which technology is used. The worst-performing sector was oil and gas due to price volatility which was worsened by the full closure of non-essential travel. The ever-growing demand for technology created this pattern in Islamic equity markets. In 2020, Islamic indices outperformed their conventional counterparts (IFSB, 2021). IFSB (2021) states three main reasons for this observation. Firstly, Shariah screening provides the company with hedging benefits during the market downfall, as it ousts companies that have higher levels of conventional borrowing. Secondly, the Shariah screening made Islamic indices go towards exposing more on the technology sector, which was the strongest-performing sector in 2020; and the final reason is that the screening process resulted in Islamic indices having a minor subgroup of constituents which, on average, have higher market capitalisations and more robust fundamentals than the larger subgroup of constituents making up the equivalent conventional indices. As for Islamic funds, it is seen that in 2020, the total assets under management of Islamic funds increased by 31.9 per cent in 2020 even in the midst of the pandemic, and these funds are concentrated in three main markets: Saudi Arabia, Malaysia and Iran (IFSB, 2021).

Following is a case study to show the developments in the stock market in the pandemic.

Case Study: Stock Market of Iran in the Midst of the Pandemic

After Sudan in April 2020 declared that it was going to adopt a conventional financial system parallel to their existing Islamic economic system, Iran is now the only country in the world that operates based on an

Islamic economic system. To manage corporate sector indebtedness and market vulnerabilities in the midst of the pandemic, the Iranian government has intervened. These interventions include the following: the Central Bank of the country announced that it was giving businesses a debt moratorium of 3 months; the National Tax Administration offered late tax payment penalty waivers for a certain period; and the Central Bank of the country announced that low-profit-rate (4 per cent) financing facilities would be granted to four million business owners adversely impacted by the pandemic (Nada, 2020).

It has been reported that following the outbreak of the pandemic, the Tehran Stock Exchange (TSE) chose a different path from that of the rest of the world. While the stock markets around the world plunged, the TSE performed well. From 20 March to 21 July 2020, the value of traders increased by 625 per cent compared to that of the previous year, and in early August, the highest value was recorded (Ziya & Vatanka, 2020). In this period, even the prices of the companies that were making losses increased (Ziya & Vatanka, 2020). On 15 April 2020, in the midst of the pandemic, the government of Iran had the biggest initial public offering (IPO) that the country ever has seen by opening for the sale of the government's residual shares in 18 companies (including a 12 per cent share of the Social Welfare Fund [SHASTA], the largest public company) with the objective of generating income to manage the economy that has been adversely affected by the pandemic and U.S. sanctions (International Monetary Fund, 2021). Despite the pandemic, new companies were successfully listed on the TSA. From the TSA's official website it was found that on 19 February 2020, a total of 1,498,711 investors participated in the IPO of Padideh Shimi Gharn Co., setting a new record for public offerings in the Iranian Capital Market where 100 million equity shares were offered (Tehran Stock Exchange, 2020A); on 4 March 2020, it was reported that the first virtually held IPO at TSE was successfully concluded, where 910 million shares, equivalent to 13 per cent equity shares of Mellat Investment Bank, were offered (Tehran Stock Exchange, 2020B); on 11 March 2020, 412 million shares, representing 15 per cent of total equity shares of Kowsar Agricultural Investment Company (KAICO), were offered; as mentioned earlier, on 15 April 2020, the largest IPO of TSA took place, where 8 billion shares, representing 10 per cent of total equity shares of Shasta, were floated on TSA (Tehran Stock Exchange, 2020C); on 1 July 2020, Tamin Cement Investment Company went public (Tehran Stock Exchange, 2020D); on 8 July 2020, Parsian Leasing Co. offered

400 million shares to the public (Tehran Stock Exchange, 2020E); on 22 July 2020, Abadan Power Generation Company went public (Tehran Stock Exchange, 2020F); on 29 July 2020, the largest Iranian pasta exporter, Zar Macaron Industrial Company, went public (Tehran Stock Exchange, 2020 G); on 5 August 2020, Iran's major investment bank, Amin Investment Bank, went public (Tehran Stock Exchange, 2020 H); on 12 August 2020, Behsaz Kashaneh Tehran went public (Tehran Stock Exchange, 2020I); on 9 September 2020, Omid Construction and Development Co. went public (Tehran Stock Exchange, 2020 J); on 9 December 2020, Bouali Sina Petrochemical Co. (BSPC) went public (Tehran Stock Exchange, 2020 K); on 24 February 2021, Opal Kani Pars Mineral Processing Company went public (Tehran Stock Exchange, 2021A); on 26 May 2021, Kourosh Food Industry Company went public (Tehran Stock Exchange, 2021B); on 9 June 2021, Karafarin Leasing Co. went public (Tehran Stock Exchange, 2021C); on 16 June 2021, the Capital Value Management Group, the Financial Holding of the Civil Servants Pension Fund (CSPF), went public (Tehran Stock Exchange, 2021D); and on 14 July 2021, Sepidmakian Company went public (Tehran Stock Exchange, 2021E).

Sukuk Market

In the beginning of the pandemic, the view was that the sukuk market might be slow (Fitch Ratings, 2020). However, in the midst of the pandemic, it was realised that sukuk is an alternative way to raise financing for sovereigns and financial institutions that are adversely affected due to the pandemic. It has been said that the year 2020 was a record-breaking year for sukuk issuance compared to the previous year, and it has maintained its attractiveness despite the challenging times created due to the pandemic (International Islamic Financial Market, 2021). It is reported that in 2020, the total global issuance including long-term and short-term sukuk is USD 174.641 billion, which is the highest value of yearly sukuk issuances to date (International Islamic Financial Market, 2021). In the year 2019, the amount was USD 145.702 billion (International Islamic Financial Market, 2021). Therefore, in the year 2020, the sukuk issuance showed an increase of around 19.84 per cent (International Islamic Financial Market, 2021). The reason for this growth is due to the sukuk issuances from the governments in GCC, Africa, Asia and other regions, and in terms of volume of sukuk issuances, Malaysia is the leading jurisdiction, followed by other countries such as Indonesia, UAE,

Saudi Arabia and Turkey (International Islamic Financial Market, 2021). The short-term sukuk issuances were more than the long-term sukuk issuances in 2020 (International Islamic Financial Market, 2021). In the midst of the pandemic, digitalization of sukuk and linking sukuk with sustainability and achieving social objectives took place. It is seen that in 2020, the sukuk market was resilient, and the global total outstanding of sukuk stood at USD 703 billion in 2020. However, it is imperative to note that in terms of total issuance of sukuk in 2020, a 4 per cent drop was seen, where the total issuance of sukuk in 2019 was at USD 171.1 billion while in 2020 it was at USD 163.4 billion (IFSB, 2021). It was also found that the overall sukuk issuances in GCC from countries like Saudi Arabia, Kuwait, Bahrain, the United Arab Emirates, Oman, Qatar and Iran boosted the sukuk market in the region, while a slight decline in sukuk issuances was recorded in the Asian region (IFSB, 2021). The sovereign sukuk issuances in 2020 also saw a slight drop as it was at 56 per cent in 2019, while in 2020 it was at 53 per cent, and the reason for this could be due to economic shock and deep economic recession triggered by the pandemic, which was further worsened by the sharp decline in oil prices in some countries (IFSB, 2021). As for corporate sukuk, a slight drop of 1 per cent is evident, as in 2019 it was at 36 per cent while in 2020 it was 35 per cent (IFSB, 2021). In 2020, Saudi Arabia was the biggest sovereign sukuk issuer followed by Indonesia, Malaysia and Kuwait (IFSB, 2021). As for the corporate sukuk issuances, Malaysia was the biggest corporate sukuk issuer, though their issuance in 2020 was lower than that of 2019, followed by the United Arab Emirates, Saudi Arabia and Turkey (IFSB, 2021). Egypt, Uzbekistan, Algeria, Mauritius and South Africa plan to enter the sukuk market soon, while the United Kingdom has returned to the market (IFSB, 2021). It is also found that sectors that were affected by the pandemic due to containment measures taken saw a decrease in sukuk issuances (IFSB, 2021). Green and socially responsible investment (SRI) sukuk was also issued during the pandemic, and they are issued by countries like Indonesia, Saudi Arabia, the United Arab Emirates and Malaysia. The green sukuk is issued by the government of Indonesia, corporations from Malaysia and Saudi Electric Company, while environment, social and governance (ESG) linked sukuk is issued by Etihad Airways and Islamic Development Bank. The green sukuk issued in 2020 includes investment-grade USD-denominated sukuk. The new countries that entered the sukuk market include Maldives (Islamic Finance News, 2021) and Bangladesh (Al Mamun and Nabi, 2021). Despite all these positive developments in the sukuk market in the midst of the pandemic, there are also liquidity issues that were faced by obligors/issuers of some of the sukuks already issued prior to the pandemic. Due to lockdown measures, some sectors of the economy came to a halt, reducing the revenue of the businesses. For instance, the airlines industry is one of the most deeply affected industries; prior to the pandemic, Malaysian Airlines, the national carrier of Malaysia, and Garuda Indonesia also issued a sukuk. It was reported in 2020 that due to disruption caused to the airline industry, there were cash flow issues that were triggered, causing both Malaysian Airlines and Garuda Indonesia to take necessary steps by consulting the sukukholders to avoid default. In this regard, Garuda Indonesia obtained majority consent from the sukukholders to extend the maturity of the sukuk which was supposed to mature in the year 2020 by three years, while Malaysian Airlines postponed the payment it owed to the sukukholders in 2020 by six months, which is until March 2021 (Islamic Corporation for the Development of the Private Sector and REFINITIV, 2020). Unfortunately, even with the precautionary steps taken to avoid default, Garuda Indonesia sukuk defaulted in June 2021.

Following are two case studies to illustrate how technology and sustainability are linked with sukuk in the midst of the pandemic and a case study to show the impact of the pandemic on the sukuks already issued prior to the pandemic.

CASE STUDY 1: SUKUK PRIHATIN OF MALAYSIA

Sukuk Prihatin, issued by the government of Malaysia, is the first digital sukuk issued in the country in the midst of the pandemic to financially assist the recovery of the economy under the National Recovery Plan (PENJANA) (Kementerian Kewangan Malaysia, 2020). Sukuk Prihatin was launched on 5 June 2020, and the objectives of issuing this sukuk are to empower the citizens, propel business and strengthen the economy (Kementerian Kewangan Malaysia, 2020). This sukuk is a digital and retail sukuk where the minimum subscription/application amount is just RM 500, offering a profit rate of 2.0 per cent per annum, which is expected to be paid quarterly over a two-year term. The subscription to this sukuk is enabled via digital channels through JomPAY (a national initiative, supported by banks, to enable online bill payments across Malaysia) or DuitNow (a digital way to send money instantly on a 24/7 basis to mobile numbers, NRIC numbers, or business registration numbers and also receive funds instantly) on all distribution banks' digital (internet/mobile) banking. The proceeds of this sukuk are used by Kumpulan Wang COVID-19 to finance measures announced in the economic stimulus packages and recovery plan to address the COVID-19 crisis. Some of these areas include medical expenditure related to COVID-19 disease; for financing/grants for micro enterprises; and to enhance connectivity to rural schools, which will also act as hubs to connect nearby villages (Kementerian Kewangan Malaysia, 2020). The Sukuk Prihatin was oversubscribed, hitting RM 666 million, as the amount that it was intended to raise was just RM 500 million (New Straits Times, 2020). Due to this overwhelming support for the Sukuk Prihatin, on 20 September 2020, it was also reported that the government of Malaysia plans to roll out an additional amount of RM 166 million Sukuk Prihatin new sukuk issuance, of which the proceeds will be used to enhance connectivity to rural schools, support research on infectious diseases, and finance microentrepreneurs (New Straits Times, 2020).

CASE STUDY 2: SUSTAINABILITY SUKUK OF ISLAMIC DEVELOPMENT BANK (IsDB)

The largest USD public issuance of IsDB was made through issuance of Sustainability Sukuk, where USD 2.5 billion was raised in March 2021 under a USD 25 billion Trust Certificate Issuance Programme (Islamic Development Bank, 2021). The tenure of this sukuk is 5 years, where the sukuk was priced at par with a profit rate of 1.262 per cent, which would be paid on a semi-annual basis (Islamic Development Bank, 2021). The proceeds of the Sustainability Sukuk are required to be allocated to finance/refinance green (10 per cent) and social development projects (90 per cent) that are eligible under the IsDB's Sustainable Finance Framework. The Sustainable Finance Framework of IsDB has been developed in line with the Green Bond Standards, Social Bond Standards and Sustainability Bond Guidelines published by the International Capital Market Association (ICMA). Under this USD 25 billion Trust Certificate Issuance Programme, the debut issuance was made in June 2020, where USD 1.5 billion was raised (Islamic Development Bank, 2020A). The tenure of this sukuk also was 5 years, and it was priced at par with a profit rate of 0.908 per cent, which is to be paid on a semi-annual basis (Islamic Development Bank, 2020A). Unlike the 2021 sukuk issued, the proceeds from the debut Sustainability issuance is exclusively deployed by IsDB towards social projects under IsDB's Sustainable Finance Framework, with a focus on the 'access to essential services' and 'SME financing and employment generation' categories under the umbrellas of 'SDG-3: Good Health and Well-Being' and 'SDG-8: Decent Work and Economic Growth' for its 57 Member Countries, to assist them in tackling the aftermath of the COVID-19 pandemic (Islamic Development Bank, 2020A).

CASE STUDY 3: DEFAULT OF GARUDA AIRLINE'S SUKUK

In 2015, Garuda Airline of Indonesia issued the country's first corporate global sukuk out of Indonesia, and it was also the country's debut U.S. dollar offering by a company where also for the very first time sukuk issuance utilised the airline capacity structure (as part of a sukuk-al-wakala structure) in Asia (Reksodiputro, 2015). This sukuk was listed on the Singapore Stock Exchange, and it was issued on 3 June 2015 for a period of 5 years with a fixed annual profit rate of 5.95 per cent, which is paid every 6 months commencing from 3 December 2015 until 3 June 2020 (Nurdiana, 2021). It is reported that as of 31 December 2019, the outstanding balance of this sukuk reached USD 498.99 million (Nurdiana, 2021; Garuda Indonesia, 2015). Originally, though, this sukuk was supposed to be matured in the year 2020, and the sukuk was restructured by extending the maturity period by three years (The Start, 2021). In June 2021, the airline announced that it will not be able to pay the coupon payment it owes to the sukukholders after giving a 14-day grace period. The reason stated for the inability was that due to the pandemic, the airline's financial situation was extremely adversely affected, as the pandemic has suppressed air travel around the world (The Start, 2021; Nurdiana, 2021). It is reported that in February 2020, the number of inter-national passengers declined from 193,380 to just 8,967 a year later, and towards the end of 2020, the total liabilities of the company ballooned to USD 10.36 billion against USD 9.9 billion in assets (Guild, 2021).

3.2 Impact of COVID-19 on Islamic Social Finance

Unlike Islamic commercial finance, there is limited data available about the progress and impact of Islamic social finance institutions and products. The reason for this could be because, unlike Islamic commercial institutions, institutions dealing with Islamic social finance do not have specific regulatory authorities that regulate them and require them to follow certain governance standards. As such, even the developments that took place in different parts of the world in the pandemic and the impact of Islamic social finance institutions and products are not reported in a comprehensive manner.

3.2.1 Zakat

During the pandemic, zakat collection and disbursement modes have been changed from offline to online modes in many countries, and zakat has been used as an effective tool to eliminate poverty. Following are some case studies to show how zakat has been used in the midst of the pandemic as an effective Islamic social finance tool.

CASE STUDY 1: HOUSE OF ZAKAT AND WAQF UGANDA (HZWU)

House of Zakat and Waqf Uganda (HZWU) is a non-denominational and not-for-profit organization set up to manage and administer Zakat (obligatory dues) and preservation of Waqf (endowment) in accordance with Islam for the social well-being of Muslims and development of Islam. In the midst of the pandemic, HZWU used innovation to structure zakat assistance programs for those who were adversely affected by the lockdown measures taken by the government to contain the virus. Like in other parts of the world, the number of poor and needy increased even in Uganda, and HZWU believed that innovation is required to assist the population (World Zakat Forum & Badan Amil Zakat Nasional (BAZNAS), 2020). As such, HZWU introduced the 'Zakat Food Care Programme'. Further, the classical physical methods of zakat collection were also changed to online modes where the zakat payments now are accepted by HZWU via internet banking, mobile money, web checkout using Mastercard and Visa, and money transfer (World Zakat Forum & Badan Amil Zakat Nasional (BAZNAS), 2020). It is reported that from January to March 2020, the zakat collections received were considered as regular, like before the pandemic; but since March a decline in the collection of zakat was seen by HZWU (World Zakat Forum & Badan Amil Zakat Nasional (BAZNAS), 2020). The objective of the 'Zakat Food Care Programme' was to assist food shortage issues in the local communities for low-income earners by providing food packages. In total, 60 tonnes of maise, wheat flour, sugar and beans were distributed to 6,000 families in the 20 districts. The total distribution for the Zakat Food Care Programme stands at USD 50,000 to the time of this report. In this period, the fuqara and masakin make 85 per cent of the asnafs and transporting them door to door to those who are in need in twenty districts of the country (World Zakat Forum & Badan Amil Zakat Nasional (BAZNAS), 2020).

CASE STUDY 2: ZAKAT HOUSE KUWAIT

Under Law Number 5 of 1982, Zakat House Kuwait was formed on 16 January 1982 as a public authority with an independent budget and a legal personality, and it is an institution supervised by the Minister of Awqaf and Islamic Affairs. During the pandemic, Zakat House Kuwait has used zakat to assist those in need who fall within the categories of legal recipients of zakat. It is reported that from the beginning of the pandemic Zakat House of Kuwait has activated online communication channels to create awareness and promote activities conducted by the organization and used social media extensively, enabling the public to pay alms and donations through electronic platforms (World Zakat Forum & Badan Amil Zakat Nasional (BAZNAS), 2020). Like in other parts of the world, due to pandemic containment measures, many Kuwaitis lost their income and were unable to pay their monthly rent. As such, Zakat House Kuwait used zakat to pay the rentals for a 6-month period for those who are eligible to receive among the affected population in this regard (World Zakat Forum & Badan Amil Zakat Nasional (BAZNAS), 2020). Other than this, zakat cash assistance was distributed to those registered as asnaf in the database of the organization during the time of lockdown (World Zakat Forum & Badan Amil Zakat Nasional (BAZNAS), 2020). Further, the Zakat House Kuwait also contributed 70,000.00 Kuwaiti dinars to construct an emergency hospital specialised for COVID-19, covering the quarantine costs as well (World Zakat Forum & Badan Amil Zakat Nasional (BAZNAS), 2020). On 15 July 2021, it was also reported that Zakat House Kuwait has contributed through the United Nations High Commissioner for Refugees (UNHCR) to assist in the pandemic in Bangladesh in projects related to education, relief and health and to assist in the protection of Malian refugees in Mauritania, benefiting more than sixty thousand people (UNHCR, 2021).

CASE STUDY 3: THE NATIONAL AMIL ZAKAT AGENCY (BAZNAS), INDONESIA

The National Amil Zakat Agency (BAZNAS) is the official and only body established by the government based on the Decree of the President of the Republic of Indonesia No. 8 of 2001 which has the function of collecting and distributing zakat, infaq and alms (ZIS) at the national level. The enactment of Law Number 23 of 2011 on Zakat Management further strengthens the role of BAZNAS as an institution authorized to manage zakat nationally. Even before the pandemic, BAZNAS has introduced numerous digital platforms to collect zakat, and social media platforms have been used to promote zakat awareness (World Zakat Forum & Badan Amil Zakat Nasional (BAZNAS), 2020). To deal with poverty and social issues in the midst of the pandemic, BAZNAS has introduced health emergency and socioeconomic emergency programs where the zakat has been distributed to more than five million people and the zakat funds distributed amount to about USD 4 million (World Zakat Forum & Badan Amil Zakat Nasional (BAZNAS), 2020).

CASE STUDY 4: NATIONAL ZAKAT FOUNDATION (NZF), UK

National Zakat Foundation (NZF) is a national charity (Charity number: 1153719) which enables local Muslims to connect their zakat to those who need it in the UK by providing support to individuals and families in need through grants for hardship relief, housing and work, and education. NZF also helps educate zakat givers about calculating and giving zakat correctly. It is reported that in 2020, due to pandemic, the zakat collection which was done physically was changed to a full online system that could be used not only by givers, but also by the recipients and the team managing the foundation (National Zakat Foundation, 2021). The Foundation distributed GBP£ 3.8 million as zakat received from more than 7,000 payers to more than 13,426 recipients, which is twice more than the number of recipients who received zakat in 2019 (National Zakat Foundation, 2021). Among these 13,426 recipients, 11,301 were given zakat under the hardship fund; 1,980 recipients were given zakat under the housing and work fund; and 145 students received it under the education fund. It is also reported that in the later part of 2020, due to the high demand for zakat, the Foundation was facing a shortage of zakat money. As such, the Foundation made an appeal to the public by launching the "Zakat is running out" campaign, which received overwhelming response and provided the Foundation with enough funding to distribute zakat to all recipients who needed it (National Zakat Foundation, 2021). The purpose of the hardship relief fund is to provide zakat relief in the UK to those who are living in hardship to cover basic needs, while the purpose of the housing and work fund is to provide support to live in an "affordable, liveable and safe accommodation" (National Zakat Foundation, 2021). The education fund of the Foundation provides support for education and training needs (National Zakat Foundation, 2021).

3.2.2 Sadaqat

During the pandemic, sadaqat or infaq are activated in some countries to assist those who are adversely affected by the pandemic. Instead of relying on the physical collection and disbursement of charity received, online modes have been used as well. Not only this, but the marketing campaigns also have been changed to online modes. There have also been some initiatives to find volunteers to offer help in the pandemic who are given the opportunity to assist virtually. What follows are some case studies presented to show how sadaqat or infaq have been used in the midst of the pandemic as an effective Islamic social finance tool.

CASE STUDY 1: VOLUNTEERS.AE INITIATIVE

Volunteers.ae was launched in Abu Dhabi, United Arab Emirates (UAE) to gather volunteers to help in the midst of the pandemic in any project that needs assistance by providing such opportunities virtually. It is a partnership between the Emirates Foundation and the Ministry of Community Development. A "virtual majlis" or a virtual platform is provided to share international experiences from experts to overcome the pandemic challenges faced. Volunteering and virtual volunteering opportunities can be requested from this website. There are numerous benefits for volunteers, volunteer groups and organizations. The benefits for volunteers include opportunities to obtain seed funding for innovative volunteer ideas, the chance to take up a volunteer activity that suits the interest and skillset of the volunteer, the chance to create an experience record for volunteering, awards recognizing volunteering efforts, and the assurance of volunteering hours being accredited and documented. Benefits for volunteer groups include obtaining transcripts and reports which are accredited, opportunities to get specialized volunteers, call center and customer support services, marketing of volunteering activities and projects, and organising of round-table sessions for purposes of knowledge exchange. The benefits for organizations include opportunities to create electronic volunteer management systems and chances to manage volunteer projects and recruit volunteers. Currently, more than sixty volunteer projects are listed on the website.

CASE STUDY 2: "100 MILLION MEALS" INITIATIVE

The "100 Million Meals" initiative is an extension of the "10 Million Meals" campaign that was launched locally in UAE in the year 2020 by UAE-based Mohammed bin Rashid Al Maktoum Global Initiatives (MBRGI) to support communities adversely affected by COVID-19. The assistance through this initiative was provided during the month of Ramadhan to disadvantaged individuals and families residing in 20 countries. The "100 Million Meals" initiative is being promoted as the biggest food drive initiative in the region. The vision of this initiative is to increase the UAE's unabating efforts to develop effective and practical results to fight poverty and hunger, which are two critical obstacles facing humanity. The partners of this initiative are Mohammed bin Rashid Al Maktoum Humanitarian and Charity Establishment, Food Banking Regional Network, United Nations World Food Programme and the Islamic Affairs and Charitable Activities Department in Dubai. Though this initiative is closed for now, a total of

216,061,671 meals were donated through it. The World's Tallest Donation Box initiative also was launched in conjunction with the "100 Million Meals" initiative where companies and individuals could purchase lights for AED 10 each to provide nutritious food to those adversely affected by the pandemic in the country. The ultimate goal of this initiative was to provide 1.2 million meals by illuminating a staggering 1.2 million lights on the façade of Burj Khalifa in an astounding exhibition of cohesion and social solidarity.

CASE STUDY 3: MERCY MALAYSIA'S COVID-19 PANDEMIC FUND
MERCY Malaysia or Malaysian Medical Relief Society is a non-profit organisation registered under Societies Act 1966 of Malaysia that targets on giving medical relief, sustainable health-related developmen and risk-reduction activities for vulnerable communities in both crisis and non-crisis situations. MERCY Malaysia launched its COVID-19 pandemic fund to support the essential needs of marginalised groups and provide medical services. The aid assistances and deliverables in this fund are assisted by the Ministry of Health, the National Crisis Preparedness and Response Centre (CPRC), and the National Agency for Disaster Management (NADMA). As of 27 August 2021, the amount of donations received was RM 64,896,558 and the amount spent was RM 41,314,685 (MERCY Malaysia, 2021). Through this pandemic fund, the assistances provided include 33,024 isolation coveralls, 106,507 isolation gowns, 49,502 aprons, 15,200 metres of non-woven fabric, 73,210 face shields, 184, 260 shoe covers, 99,210 head covers, 512,259 face masks, 337,008 gloves, 34,428 hand sanitizers, 667 thermometers, 65 ventilators, 7.975 ventilators, 31 intubation boxes, 7,310 food vouchers and RM 200,000 cash assistance (MERCY Malaysia, 2021).

3.2.3 Waqf

During the pandemic, waqf has also been used to provide relief for those adversely affected by the pandemic. Instead of relying on the classical ways of waqf, innovative waqf products also have been innovated. In this regard, waqf-linked sukuk is an innovative product that needs to be highlighted. Waqf institutions have also provided assistance in cash and kind in the midst of the pandemic. Following are some case studies to show how waqf has been used in the midst of the pandemic as an effective Islamic social finance tool.

CASE STUDY 1: INDONESIA'S PANDEMIC RETAIL CASH WAQF-LINKED SUKUK

On 9 October 2020, the government of Indonesia issued a retail cash waqf-linked sukuk to finance the recovery of an economy hit by the pandemic (Winosa, 2020). The subscription for this sukuk was closed on 12 November 2020. Sukukholders can purchase a sukuk for minimum IDR 1 million (USD 68) with no maximum limit prescribed through any of the sukuk distribution partners: BRI Syariah, Bank Syariah Mandiri, BNI Syariah and Bank Muamalat (Winosa, 2020). This sukuk was based on the Wakalah (agency) structure. The sukuk was guaranteed by the government of Indonesia and could not be traded in the secondary market. The tenure of the sukuk was only for two years with a fixed profit of 5.5 per cent per year. There were two types of sukukholders, as the sukukholders could become participants of either a temporary waqf or a perpetual waqf. The difference is that, in a temporary waqf arrangement, the sukukholder would get back their principal amount and would give the manager of the waqf the return generated from the sukuk to manage the identified social projects. However, in the case of the perpetual waqf arrangement, both the principal and the return from the sukuk were given by the sukukholders to the manager of the waqf to use for the identified social projects that included education, health and economic empowerment. The total sukuk proceeds collected from this issuance were IDR 24.141 billion (USD 1,694,812), of which IDR 15.661 billion were contributed by 588 retail sukukholders, while IDR 8.48 billion were contributed by three institutional sukukholders.

CASE STUDY 2: WAKAF SELANGOR MUAMALAT AND WAKAF NEGERI SEMBILAN MUAMALAT, MALAYSIA

During the pandemic in the year 2020, Wakaf Selangor Muamalat contributed RM 369,200.00 to 18 selected hospitals in Malaysia (Wakaf Muamalat, 2020). The donations included medical equipment such as syringe pump machines, N95 face masks and personal protective equipment (PPE) for frontline health workers dealing with the spread of the COVID-19 outbreak (Wakaf Muamalat, 2020). In July 2021, Wakaf Negeri Sembilan Muamalat donated 5 patient transport trolleys and 10 oxygen concentrators to the State Health Department, Negeri Sembilan (JKNNS) (Wakaf Muamalat, 2021). The total value of these items was RM 81,500.00 (Wakaf Muamalat, 2021). This contribution was made based on the current COVID-19 situation in Negeri Sembilan, where the majority of patients need oxygen assistance.

CASE STUDY 3: RUMAH WAQAF, INDONESIA

Rumah Zakah of Indonesia also operates a Rumah Waqaf which administrates cash and real assets under the Gelombang (Wave) Waqf program. In the midst of the pandemic, cash waqf was used to assist the poor and needy in a number of ways. For instance, it is reported that these funds were used to provide water wells for the poor, an aromatic coconut garden, mosques, madrasah (Islamic schools), mini markets, food barns, a clove factory and vegetable gardens, and funds were also used for sheep fattening and renting houses (IFSB, 2021). At the same time, Qurans and ventilators for COVID-19 patients were given (IFSB, 2021). Not only this, using these funds, interest-free loans were provided to micro-entrepreneurs (IFSB, 2021). Overall, it is reported that using these waqf funds, 500,000 beneficiaries in 28 cities in 18 provinces of Indonesia received assistance (IFSB, 2021).

3.2.4 Islamic Microfinance

During the pandemic, Islamic microfinance institutions have also played an imperative role in assisting low-income groups of the population to survive and have a means to receive sustainable income. Following are some case studies to show how waqf has been used in the midst of the pandemic as an effective Islamic social finance tool.

CASE STUDY 1: AKHUWAT PAKISTAN

Akhuwat is an Islamic microfinance institution, established in Pakistan, which is based on four pillars: iman (faith), ihsan (to do beautiful things), ikhlas (purity) and infaq (charity). Today, Akhuwat has chapters formed in different parts of the world including the USA. The unique model of Akhuwat emphasizes creating bonds of solidarity between the affluent and the marginalised. Applicants for interest-free loans are required to have guarantors, and upon successfully receiving the interest-free loans they are encouraged to become givers of funds by making a small donation, which is 2 cents a day (IFSB, 2021). From the beginning of the pandemic, specific programs to alleviate poverty caused by adverse impact of the lockdown measures adopted by the government were inaugurated. In this regard, Akhuwat has set up a "Corona Imdadi Fund" with the objective of assisting disregarded segments of the society in the pandemic. The objectives of this fund are to provide ration packages, free coronavirus testing service, a professional consulting helpline and support for hospitals where facilities are inadequate (Pakistan Centre for

Philanthropy, 2020). As of April 2020, they were able to collect PKR 3.56 million through donations, while their target is to raise PKR 10 million in total (Pakistan Centre for Philanthropy, 2020). It is stated that using these funds, USD 95,000 worth of grants have been distributed to 5,703 beneficiaries, 234,311 meals have been distributed, USD 3 million has been disbursed as interest-free loans to 34,631 beneficiaries, and 132,417 ration bags have been distributed (Akhwat USA, 2020).

CASE STUDY 2: AMANAH IKHTIAR MALAYSIA (AIM)

AIM is an Islamic microfinance institution operating in Malaysia, and in the midst of the pandemic, to assist its members in repaying loans/financing facilities given without being in default, debt moratoriums were granted. Due to the lockdown measures taken by the government, the majority of economic activities were stopped and the incomes of many AIM members also were adversely affected. It is reported that 262,000 members nationwide in the country benefited from the moratoriums (Utusan Malaysia, 2020). The debt moratorium was effective immediately for a period of five weeks from November 9 to December 6, 2020 with a three-time deferral process and a maximum additional moratorium of one year (Utusan Malaysia, 2020). Apart from this, AIM also introduced a "Love Basket" (Bakul Kasih) program, where essential supplies were delivered during the lockdown period to members who needed them. On 9 November 2020, it was reported that AIM had delivered 1,500 such baskets (Utusan Malaysia, 2020).

3.2.5 Social Takaful

During the pandemic, social takaful has been activated in some countries to assist the low-income population. However, among Islamic social finance products and services, the least used and/or reported one is social takaful. This could be due to lack of awareness about the potential of takaful as a social finance product. Following is a case study presented to show how social takaful in the midst of the pandemic is an effective Islamic social finance tool.

CASE STUDY: MYSALAM COMMUNITY PROTECTION TAKAFUL SCHEME FROM MALAYSIA

The mySalam Community protection takaful is a Shariah-compliant scheme that, due to the pandemic, was not designed and introduced.

However, it was an ongoing scheme that was in the community prior to the pandemic and was utilized during the pandemic to assist the community. The mySalam community protection scheme is a government initiative that aims to provide free takaful health coverage to 6.8 million Malaysians who are eligible to receive it. There are two categories of eligible recipients: recipients in Bantuan Sara Hidup register aged between 18 to 65, and Bantuan Sara Hidup (BSH) recipients.

Bantuan Sara Hidup register aged between 18 to 65 who are eligible for mySalam takaful coverage include individuals aged between 18 and 65 with spouse, single individuals aged between 40 and 65 with an income of less than RM 24,000 per annum, and disabled individuals aged between 18 and 65 with an income of less than RM 24,000 per annum. mySalam benefits for BSH recipients are a one-time payment for a critical illness claim of RM 8,000 plus a hospitalisation benefit of RM 50, for a maximum of 14 days per annum. These protections under mySalam are provided for free to eligible recipients. The Great Eastern Holdings (GEH) Limited has injected RM 2 billion for this scheme, and it is anticipated that these injected funds will last for 5 years.

In the midst of the pandemic, the mySalam takaful scheme was extended to those affected by the pandemic. The protection has been extended to individuals who are quarantined at home or at the COVID-19 Quarantine and Treatment Center (PKRC) (Manzor, 2021). Not only this, but Malaysians who are eligible under the mySalam takaful scheme and are hospitalised due to the COVID-19 virus can claim a hospital allowance of RM 50 a day for up to 14 days a year, and complications due to the COVID-19 virus that result in any of the 45 listed critical illnesses can make a claim under the Critical Illness benefit.

4 Reforms Required for a Resilient Islamic Finance Industry in a Post-COVID Era

The pandemic has provided Islamic finance with the opportunity to re-strategize the industry in light of the challenges faced. Here we list the eight reforms required in this regard to create a resilient Islamic finance industry in a post-COVID era.

4.1 Convergence of Islamic Social Finance with Islamic Commercial Finance

One of the challenges detected in the midst of the pandemic was the inadequacy of Islamic commercial finance to deal with customers whose income was adversely affected. To provide assistance to them, the financing options available would be from modes of Islamic social finance such as zakat, sadaqat/infaq, waqf, takaful and Islamic microfinance. As such, it is realised that convergence of Islamic social finance with Islamic commercial finance is needed. The model that should be followed in this regard is to create the opportunity for Islamic financial institutions focussing on Islamic commercial finance to offer Islamic social finance as well. Figure 1 illustrates the proposed model.

4.2 Escalating the Adoption of Technology in Offering Islamic Finance Products and Services

Islamic financial institutions, like conventional financial institutions, need to escalate the adoption of technology in offering Islamic financial products and services. In the midst of the pandemic, it has been realised that there is a need to find an alternative to the physical presence of customers required to obtain financial products and services. Via adoption of technology, electronic Know Your Customer (KYC) procedures can be adopted, and the financial products and services can be offered in a socially distant manner through online platforms created for the purpose. However, it is essential to note that adoption of technology without proper rules and guidelines could be a risk, and therefore policymakers and regulatory authorities need to enact proper rules and

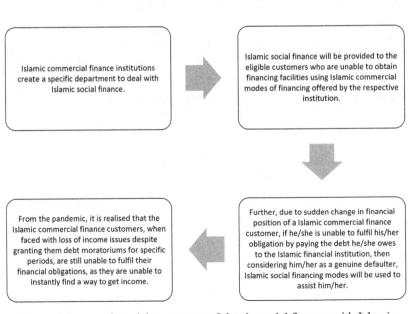

Figure 1 Proposed model to converge Islamic social finance with Islamic commercial finance

Policy makers, including the regulatory authorities, need to create the enabling legal, regulatory and governance infrastructure to adopt technology.

• Different countries have progressed at different paces in this regard and therefore, it is imperative to assess the required developments needed and to enact the required rules prior to the adoption of technology by the Islamic financial institutions. This is essential to have certainty in the business environment and to protect customers.

Internal regulations to adopt technology and to regulate the business transactions need to be enacted by the Islamic financial institutions.

• Adoption of technology in Islamic financial institutions is not free from risks. As such, to mitigate the new risks that will emerge due to the use of technology, proper codification of internal regulations in line with corporate governance is required. This is to ensure that there is a proper procedure put in place to handle uncertainties and risks arising from new ways adopted in providing Islamic finance products and services.

Figure 2 Special considerations in adopting technology to offer Islamic finance products and services

guidelines that would regulate the adoption of technology by Islamic financial institutions. For instance, issuance of digital banking licenses could be escalated with proper rules and guidelines. Figure 2 illustrates the special considerations that need to be addressed in escalating the adoption of technology in offering Islamic finance products and services.

4.3 Linking Islamic Finance with Achieving the United Nations' Sustainable Development Goals

The pandemic has resulted in an increase in the global poverty level and has turned back the world poverty clock. Therefore, there is a need to redouble efforts to achieve the United Nations' sustainable development goals. There is no doubt that Islamic finance can play an important role in this regard. For instance, if the full potential of zakat could be unlocked, the poor and needy could be assisted. However, the challenge here is to formulate a way in which the full potential of Islamic finance modes can be unlocked to link them with the United Nations' sustainable development goals. Figure 3 illustrates the strategy that could be adopted in Islamic finance to link it with the United Nations' sustainable development goals.

4.4 Creating a Value-Based Intermediation Approach in Offering Islamic Finance Products and Services

Profit maximization should not be the only goal of Islamic financial institutions. The impact that the financial products and services have on society and the environment also needs to be considered. Islamic finance products and services

Islamic financial institutions need to adopt a yearly target to achieve the United Nations' sustainable development goals.

- The Islamic financial institutions need to set yearly targets to achieve in attaining the United Nations' sustainable development goals. In structuring Islamic finance products and services, Islamic financial institutions need to consider the impact that those products and services will have on the society.

Islamic financial institutions need to measure and report continuously the way they have achieved the United Nations' sustainable development goals.

- What is being achieved by the Islamic financial institutions in this regard needs to be measured and reported to the public in a continuous manner. This could be done in the website and the annual report of the respective Islamic financial institution. Using this approach, the Islamic financial institutions can improve what they do and can inspire others to do the same. Likewise, this would also help to improve the supply side of the funds by educating as well as motivating the stakeholders to participate in this cause.

International financial products to achieve the United Nations' sustainable development goals need to be created in collaboration with multilateral financial institutions and international humantarian organizations.

- One of the hiccups in unlocking the full potential of Islamic finance products and services, especially Islamic social finance products and services, is restricting those financial products and services to one geographical location. As such, a way to utilize these products and services borderlessly needs to be formulated. In this regard, multilateral organizations and international humanitarian agencies can play a leading role in issuing products and managing projects in an effective and transparent manner to achieve the target set, using their resources to reach the unreachable.

Figure 3 Proposed strategy to link Islamic finance with the United Nations' sustainable development goals

have been criticized for considering their Shariah compliance aspect only, without creating Shariah-based financial products and services that are aligned with Maqasid al Shariah (objectives of Shariah). Figure 4 provides the aspects that ought to be covered in creating value-based intermediation financial products and services offered by Islamic financial institutions.

4.5 Promoting Circular Economy Initiatives via Islamic Finance

Circular economy, also known as sustainable economy, minimizes wastage in natural resources which are limited with the aim of preserving them for upcoming generations without overexploiting them. The opposite of circular economy is linear economy, in which businesses utilize natural resources to create products which at the end become waste, as they are designed and created in such a way that recycling them is not possible. However, in a circular economy, recycling of the goods produced using the natural resources makes the process more sustainable, minimizing wastage. As such, the notion of circular economy needs to be promoted in Islamic finance. Figure 5 shows how Islamic financial institutions could promote circular economy initiatives.

4.6 Complementing Shariah Governance with Human Governance

Islamic financial institutions have to adhere to both corporate governance and Shariah governance principles to manage the way in which they operate. However, what was realised in the midst of the pandemic is that merely having

Emphasize on people, profit and planet using a balanced approach.

- Instead of focusing only on profit-oriented financial products and services, the Islamic financial institutions ought to work towards achieving financial inclusion by structuring financial products and services that are suitable for all people in societies while balancing them in protection of the planet by preserving the environment in a sustainable manner. The short-term profit-oriented financial products and services should not be given priority over the medium or long-term sustainable financial and non-financial gains.

Non-financial performance indicators are being used to measure the success of the Islamic finance institutions.

- Apart from the classical use of financial performance indicators, non-financial performation indicators ought to be introduced within Islamic financial institutions to measure their success. In this regard, the in-house Shariah advisory organs of the Islamic financial institutions also can formulate yardsticks to create value-based Islamic financial products and services which could be promoted as Shariah-based products that go beyond mere Shariah compliance.

Innovation is used to create impact-based financial products and services.

- Islamic financial products and services can be customized to the purpose using innovation and therefore, to create value-based financial products and services in the market, innovative ways can be adopted.

Stakeholders of Islamic financial institutions need to be empowered to collaborate with each other and complement each other in doing the common good.

- This means that apart from the shareholders of Islamic financial institutions, other stakeholders such as customers and staff will play a pivotal role in assisting Islamic financial institutions meet their target to create value-based financial products and services by assisting the respective financial institutions. In this regard, there shall be collaboration among the stakeholders, and each of the stakeholder groups shall complement the other in promoting the common good.

Figure 4 Aspects to be covered in creating value-based intermediation financial products and services offered by Islamic financial institutions

Have special financial products and services for customers engaged in circular economy initiatives.

Create a special financing portfolio for customers who engage in circular economy initiatives.

Introduce incentive packages for those customers engaged in circular economy initiatives which could be parallel to the policies of the governments.

Provide financing using collaboration (profit sharing arrangements) for customers promoting circular economy initiatives.

Figure 5 How Islamic financial institutions could promote circular economy initiatives

a rule-based approach to achieve ethical behaviour within the financial institutions via principles of corporate governance and Shariah governance is not enough. This is because, ultimately, the integrity and sincerity of the individuals running the financial institution matter when it comes to the practicing of ethical behaviour. As such, human governance principles have become more relevant than ever and are being adopted by Islamic financial institutions. In this regard, the Accounting and Auditing Organization for Islamic Financial Institutions (AAOIFI)'s "Code of

> An Islamic commercial finance institution will collaborate with an Islamic social finance institution like a zakat and charity institution.

> If the Islamic commercial finance institution finds a genuine defaulter, then the information about the genuine defaulter will be shared with the zakat and charity institution.

> After doing an independent assessment of the genuine defaulter referred by the Islamic commercial finance institution, if it is found that they deserve financial assistance, financial assistance will be provided to settle their debt and assist them in overcoming the financial hardship based on the case.

Figure 6 Proposed way to provide assistance by Islamic commercial financial institutions to genuine defaulters

ethics for Islamic finance professionals" can be adopted by all Islamic financial institutions. AAOIFI's Code deals with five categories of violations of ethical virtues, which are transaction related, culture related, leadership or management related, interpersonal related and personal related (AAOIFI, 2021).

4.7 Introducing an Adequate and Equitable Mechanism to Deal with Genuine Defaulters

In the midst of the pandemic, it was realised that Islamic financial institutions need to differentiate between genuine defaulters and intentional defaulters to ensure that actions taken against defaulters are just and equitable. In this regard, a practical approach needs to be adopted to where even modern technology such as Artificial Intelligence (AI) and data analytics could be used to determine who the genuine defaulters are. These individuals shall be given leniency by providing them with the opportunity to use an Islamic social finance mode such as zakat to assist them in overcoming the financial hardship they are in. It is imperative for Islamic financial institutions to add this feature to the Shariah governance framework to monitor this aspect and have an equitable and just way to deal with the situation. Further, there is a need to establish within Islamic commercial financial institutions a way to provide financial assistance to genuine defaulters. Figure 6 illustrates how this could be done.

4.8 Formulating Governance Standards for Islamic Social Finance

Islamic social finance is considered to be the informal sector of the economy, and as such, institutionalization of Islamic social finance in a unified manner is limited. Islamic microfinance institutions do utilize multiple types of Islamic social finance tools or institutions in some parts of the world. The pandemic has provided an opportunity to create Islamic social finance institutions that would provide Islamic social finance tools and institutions under one roof. However, a limitation in this regard is not having comprehensive Shariah governance standards to be followed. There are ad hoc governance standards for different tools and institutions of Islamic social finance such as zakat and waqf; but a comprehensive governance framework or standards that could be used for Islamic social finance is missing. As such, it is imperative to develop such a comprehensive standard to ensure that high standards of governance leading to strict Shariah compliance will be achieved. Further, the strategy to achieve UN SDGs, ESGs and what needs to be accomplished under the Paris Agreement to resolve climate issues using Islamic finance also needs to be elaborated. Table 3 illustrates the areas that ought to be focussed on in developing a comprehensive governance standard for Islamic social finance.

4.9 Introducing Gross Domestic Product (GDP)-Linked Sukuk to Control and Overcome Fiscal Indebtedness of Governments

A GDP-linked sukuk is a debt security on which the issuer promises to pay a return based on the Shariah contract used, which will be linked with the GDP performance of the issuing country. This concept was developed from an idea proposed by economist Martin Bailey in 1983 on transforming sovereign debt into domestic export claims (Islamic Finance News, 2013). Conventional GDP-linked bonds have been used in the world since the 1990s, when Argentina and Greece employed them successfully (Islamic Finance News, 2013). Bacha (2019) defines GDP-linked sukuk as a sukuk based on a standard contract like Ijarah, but with coupon/dividends linked to GDP growth. Due to the pandemic, governments have incurred additional debts to overcome the economic hardships caused to domestic economies by injecting funds in the form of fiscal stimulus programs. In the midst of the pandemic it was realised that governments need to find ways to manage their fiscal debts in such a way as to avoid creating additional debt obligations. Linking the sukuk to the performance of GDP of a country has a number of advantages; for example, the likelihood of default of such sukuks will be lower, and the government will not have to rely on engaging in further debts to pay off the debt. However, the volatility of GDP indicators in a country will be the ultimate decisive factor for investors to decide whether investing in such a financial security is worth the cost. This simply means the attractiveness of a GDP-linked sukuk will depend on the GDP performance of the country, and as such, not every country may be able to issue a GDP-linked sukuk. The idea is that GDP-linked sukuk

Table 3 Areas proposed to be covered in the governance standards for Islamic social finance

Area focused	Details
Board Governance	This part should cover the responsibilities, qualifications and composition of the board.
Shariah Board Governance	This part should cover the responsibilities, qualifications and composition of the Shariah organ of the institution. A Shariah board secretariat shall be established to assist the Shariah board in carrying out its functions, and the Shariah research function should be carried out by the Shariah board secretariat.
Operational Model	The operational model will be derived from Shariah rules applicable to each type of Islamic social finance tool/instrument/institution.
Shariah Internal Control Functions	The minimum Shariah internal control functions that ought to be established in the institution shall be covered in this part. The Shariah internal control functions include Shariah review, Shariah risk management and Shariah audit functions.
Transparency and Accountability	This part should govern the legal and Shariah compliance and accountability requirements that ought to be adhered to. Conducting of financial audits and utilization of institutional resources to achieve the institution's objectives must be explained. A clear scorecard or performance and output measurement methodology shall be formulated and implemented to understand where the institutions stand. The way public information will

be given through websites and other means and the publishing of annual reports shall be covered in this part.

Collecting Contributions	A convenient and responsible way to collect distribution shall be formulated and such information shall be publicly disclosed to the stakeholders.
Disbursing of Contributions	Parties to whom the contributions will be disbursed and the way they can apply to receive contributions shall be covered. An equitable and fair way of registration shall be introduced. In distributing contributions, the Shariah rules that ought to be followed in different types of Islamic social finance instruments/tools/institutions shall be followed.
Managing Contributions	A transparent way in which contributions received will be managed shall be formulated. If the money is kept in an investment bank account, what happens to the returns must be clearly discussed. To manage the contributions, a special investment and liquidity management committee shall be set up.
Strategic Collaborations and Affiliations with other Institutions	It is important to leverage strength on others to move the institution forward. As such, the way in which strategic collaborations and affiliations will be made should be made clear in this part.
Civic Engagement	It is imperative to specify the ways in which civic engagement would be performed and the level in which these engagements will be carried out.
Human Resource Management	Every institution shall have dedicated staffs to carry out its functions and no institution shall 100 per cent rely on volunteers. At minimum a financial officer or an accountant shall be hired, and how human resource management is conducted shall be made clear.

Table 3 (cont.)

Area focused	Details
Volunteers Management	The way in which volunteers will be managed shall be clear, and guidelines should be developed to manage them.
Continuous Disclosure Obligations	Quarterly impact and financial reports shall be published by the institution to boost the confidence of stakeholders in the institution.
Establishment of Hisbah (ombudsman) Institution	A hisbah institution within the institution shall be established to hear grievances and complaints lodged. Further, on their own initiative, the members appointed in the hibah shall check from time to time on whether the operations of the institution align with its objectives and rules.
Technology Governance	How technology risks are mitigated shall be covered in this part, including the scope of technology's use and the security measures taken.
Managing Operational Risks including Shariah Non-Compliance Risk	How the operational risks are managed, including Shariah non-compliance risk, shall be clearly stated. How the consequences of these risks shall be managed is important to be laid down.

could be an innovative way through which the debts of a country could be converted to equity repayments based on GDP, and therefore, COVID-19 stimulus programs of the governments ought to be financed via issuance of GDP-linked sukuk (Mohamed, 2020; Mohamed and Mobin, 2020). Mohamed (2020) highlights three main advantages of issuing GDP-linked sukuk through governments to finance pandemic stimulus programs, and they are as follows: issuing GDP-linked sukuk will give governments more fiscal space to manage their debts; linking the return to GDP will allow countries to pay returns to the sukukholders based on the economic growth of the country; and the nature of GDP-linked sukuk is similar to that of taking insurance against unprecedented events, making it the ideal financial security to be issued in the midst of the pandemic. Since debt indexation to certain indicators from the economy like GDP is considered an effective way to reduce the risk of sovereign default (Diaw et al., 2011), issuing GDP-linked sukuk in the midst of the pandemic could be a viable option for policymakers.

Glossary

Bai':	Refers to trade/sale.
Bai' Muajjal:	Refers to a deferred sale.
Conventional finance:	Refers to financial activities that are non-compliant with Shariah.
Dhulm:	Refers to oppression.
Gharamah:	Refers to penalty charges imposed for delayed payment in financing/debt settlement, without the need to prove the actual loss suffered. Gharamah shall not be recognised as income of the Islamic financial institution, and it has to be channeled to certain charitable bodies.
Gharar:	Refers to uncertainty.
Hadith:	Saying attributed to the Prophet (SAW). Categorically it includes what he said, did, or approved.
Ijarah:	Refers to lease contract.
Islamic finance:	Refers to financial activities that complies with Islamic law.
Islamic financial institutions:	Refers to institutions offering Islamic financial products and services.
Istisna':	Refers to a manufacturing contract where the specification of the manufactured item is given by the person ordering and the price of the contract is fixed.
Hisbah:	The term hisbah means an act which is performed for the common good, or with the intention of seeking a reward from God. The purpose of the Hisbah institution is to protect members of the society from deviance, preserve their faith and guarantee the welfare of the people in both religious and worldly matters according to the Shariah.
Maysir:	Refers to gambling.

Murabahah: Refers to a trust sale where the seller of the Shariah-compliant asset should disclose the cost price and the profit before the sale takes place.

Mudharabah: Refers to an equity contract where one party provides capital, while the other party manages a Shariah-compliant business activity and both partners shall agree to a pre-agreed profit-sharing ration, while in case of loss all the financial losses shall be borne by the capital provider.

Musharakah: Refers to an equity contract where the partners agree to conduct a Shariah-compliant activity with each other by agreeing to the terms of participating in the business where a pre-agreed profit-sharing ratio shall be agreed and, in case of loss, loss shall follow the capital contribution made by the partners.

Qard: Refers to a loan where no amount of interest is charged.

Quran: The Holy Book of Muslims.

Riba: Refers to usury. There are two types of riba: riba arising from loan contract; and riba that arises due to exchange of ribawi commodities.

Ribawi commodities: The ribawi commodities are gold, silver, barley, wheat, dates and salt.

Salam: Refers to Shariah-compliant forward sale.

Shariah: The practical divine law deduced from its legitimate sources: the Quran, Sunnah, consensus, analogy and other approved sources of Islamic law.

Shariah audit: Refers to a function that provides an independent assessment of the quality and effectiveness of the IFI's internal control, risk management systems and governance processes, as well as the overall compliance of the Islamic financial institution's

	operations, business, affairs and activities with Shariah.
Shariah governance:	Refers to the manner in which Shariah compliance is achieved.
Shariah non-compliance risk:	An operational risk resulting from non-compliance of the institution with the rules and principles of Shariah in its products and services.
Shariah review:	Refers to a function that conducts regular assessment on the compliance of the operations, business, affairs and activities of the Islamic financial institution with Shariah requirements.
Shariah risk management:	Refers to a function that systematically identifies, measures, monitors and reports Shariah non-compliance risks in the operations, business, affairs and activities of the Islamic financial institution.
Sukuk:	Certificates that represent a proportional undivided ownership right in tangible assets, or a pool of tangible assets and other types of assets.
Sunnah:	Path or method. With respect to sayings, it is synonymous to hadith.
Ta'widh:	Refers to a claim for compensation arising from actual loss suffered by the financier due to delayed payment of the financing/debt amount by the customer. Islamic financial institutions may recognise ta'widh as income on the basis that it is charged as compensation for actual loss suffered by the institution.
Takaful:	Refers to Islamic insurance.
Tawarruq:	Refers to monetization or a tripartite sale.
Wakalah:	Refers to an agency which is a service-based contract where an agent could be appointed by a principal to do a Shariah-compliant activity by charging a fee or for free.

References

Abdul Aziz, Z. T. (2021). *The Role of Banks and Financial Institutions in Supporting National Economic Recovery*, www.theedgemarkets.com/article/role-banks-and-financial-institutions-supporting-national-economic-recovery.

Abdullah, A. (2018). *Evaluating Zakat-ul-Fitr Distribution*, www.islamicity.org/15606/evaluating-zakat-ul-fitr-distribution.

Accounting and Auditing Organization for Islamic Financial Institutions (AAOIFI). (2021). *Code of Ethics for Islamic Finance Professionals*, http://aaoifi.com/wp-content/uploads/2021/01/00-AAOIFI-Code-of-Ethics-for-Islamic-finance-Professionals-Final-Standard-Issued-CS.pdf.

Ahmed, S. Y. (2020). *Impact of COVID-19 on Performance of Pakistan Stock Exchange*, https://ssrn.com/abstract=3643316.

AIA PUBLIC Takaful Bhd. (2021). *AIA Malaysia Offers Two Free Covid-19 Coverage to Help Ease Malaysians' Concerns*, www.aia.com.my/en/about-aia/media-centre/press-releases/2021/AIA-Malaysia-offers-two-free-COVID-19-coverage-to-help-ease-Malaysians-concerns.html.

Akhwat USA. (2020). *Annual Report 2020*, Torrance, CA: Akhwat USA.

Al Mamun, M. S. & Nabi, M. G. (2021). *Sovereign Investment Sukuk in Bangladesh*, https://thefinancialexpress.com.bd/views/sovereign-investment-sukuk-in-bangladesh-1619191089.

Almonifi, Y. S. A., Ul-Rehman, S., & Gulzar, R. (2021). *The COVID-19 Pandemic Effect on the Performance of the Islamic Banking Sector in KSA: An Empirical Study of Al Rajhi Bank*, https://papers.ssrn.com/sol3/papers.cfm?abstract_id=3834859.

Al-Saati, A. (2003). The Permissible Gharar (Risk) in Classical Islamic Jurisprudence. *Journal of King Abdulaziz University: Islamic Economics*, **16**(2), 3–19.

Arif, M., Naeem, M. A., Hasan, M., Alawi, S. M., & Taghizadeh-Hesaryg, F. (2021). Pandemic Crisis versus Global Financial Crisis: Are Islamic Stocks a Safe-Haven for G7 Markets? *Economic Research-Ekonomska Istraživanja*, doi: 10.1080/1331677X.2021.1910532.

Ashraf, D., Rizwan, M. S., & Ahmad, G. (2020). *Islamic Equity Investments and the COVID-19 Pandemic*, https://ssrn.com/abstract=3611898.

Augustine, B. D. (2021). *GCC's Islamic Insurers Face Profitability Challenges in 2021*, https://gulfnews.com/business/banking/gccs-islamic-insurers-face-profitability-challenges-in-2021-1.81147054.

Bacha, O. I. (2019). *Making a Case for GDP-Linked Sukuk*, www.inceif.org/kmimpact/2019/04/23/making-a-case-for-gdp-linked-sukuk.

Bank Islam Malaysia Bhd. (2020). *Annual Report 2020*, Kuala Lumpur: Bank Islam Malaysia Bhd.

Bank Negara Malaysia. (2021). *Frequently Asked Questions on Temporary Relief Measures for Insurance Policyholders and Takaful Participants*, www.bnm.gov.my/documents/20124/914558/FAQ+for+consumers+%28ITOs+relief+measures%29+EN.pdf.

Çizakça, M. (1998). Awqaf in History and Its Implications for Modern Islamic Economies. *Islamic Economic Studies*, **6**(1), 43–70.

Diaw, A., Bacha, O. I., & Lahsasna, A. (2011). *Public Sector Funding and Debt Management: A Case for GDP-Linked Sukuk*, www.maybank2u.com.my/iwov-resources/islamic-my/document/my/en/islamic/scoe/knowledge-centre/research-paper/Public_Sector_Funding.pdf.

Dubai Islamic Bank. (2021). *Dubai Islamic Bank Full Year 2020 Group Financial Results*, www.dib.ae/about-us/news/2021/02/16/dubai-islamic-bank-full-year-2020-group-financial-results.

Erdoğan, S., Gedikli, A., & Çevik, E. I. (2020). The Effects of the Covid-19 Pandemic on Conventional and Islamic Stock Markets in Turkey. *Bilimname*, **42**(2), 89–110. doi: http://dx.doi.org/10.28949/bilimname.799413.

Fitch Rating. (2020). *Sukuk Issuance Picking Up after Coronavirus Slowdown*, www.fitchratings.com/research/islamic-finance/sukuk-issuance-picking-up-after-coronavirus-slowdown-20-07-2020.

Garuda Indonesia. (2015). *Garuda Indonesia Global Sukuk Limited*, https://secure.fundsupermart.com/fsm/bond/relatedBondDocument/XS1238157181/Offering%20Circular.pdf.

Guild, J. (2021). Is Garuda Indonesia on the Brink of Bankruptcy? www.eastasiaforum.org/2021/07/07/is-garuda-indonesia-on-the-brink-of-bankruptcy.

Hasan, A. I. & Risfandy, T. (2021). Islamic Banks' Stability: Full-Fledged vs Islamic Windows. *Journal of Accounting and Investment*, **22**(1), 192–205.

Insurance Services Malaysia Bhd. (2021). *Insurance and Takaful Industry Launches COVID-19 Test Fund*, www.ism.net.my/insurance-and-takaful-industry-launches-covid-19-test-fund.

International Islamic Financial Market. (2021). *Sukuk Report*, www.iifm.net/wp-content/uploads/2021/08/IIFM-Sukuk-Report-10th-Edition.pdf.

International Monetary Fund. (2021). *Policy Responses to COVID-19*, www.imf.org/en/Topics/imf-and-covid19/Policy-Responses-to-COVID-19#I.

Islami Bank Bangladesh Limited. (n.d.). *Rural Development Scheme*, www.islamibankbd.com/prodServices/rdsScheme.php.

Islamic Corporation for the Development of the Private Sector and REFINITIV. (2020). *Islamic Finance Development Report 2020*, https://icd-ps.org/uploads/files/ICD-Refinitiv%20IFDI%20Report%2020202016075028 93_2100.pdf.

Islamic Development Bank. (2020A). *Islamic Development Bank Issues US$ 1.5 Billion Debut Sustainability Sukuk in Response to COVID-19*, www.isdb.org/news/islamic-development-bank-issues-us-15-billion-debut-sustainability-sukuk-in-response-to-covid-19.

Islamic Development Bank. (2020B). *The Covid-19 Crisis and Islamic Finance*, Jeddah: Islamic Development Bank.

Islamic Development Bank. (2021). *Islamic Development Bank Issues Largest Sustainability Sukuk Ever*, www.isdb.org/news/islamic-development-bank-issues-largest-sustainability-sukuk-ever.

Islamic Finance News. (2013). *GDP-Linked Sukuk: The Solution to Government Debt*, http://islamicfinancenews.com/sites/default/files/newsletters/v10i41.pdf.

Islamic Finance News. (2021). *Maldives Issues the Debut Sovereign Sukuk*, www.islamicfinancenews.com/maldives-issues-debut-sovereign-sukuk.html.

Islamic Financial Services Board (IFSB). (2020A). *Assessing the Stability of the Islamic Banking Industry Amid the Covid-19 Pandemic*, IFSB Working Paper Series, WP-18/12/2020, Kuala Lumpur: Islamic Financial Services Board.

Islamic Financial Services Board (IFSB). (2020B). *Digital Transformation in Islamic Banking*, IFSB Working Paper Series, WP-19/12/2020, Kuala Lumpur: Islamic Financial Services Board.

Islamic Financial Services Board (IFSB). (2021). *Islamic Financial Services Industry Stability Report 2021*, Kuala Lumpur: Islamic Financial Services Board.

Islamic Research and Training Institute, Islamic Development Bank. (2020). *Islamic Social Finance Report 2020*, Jeddah: Islamic Development Bank.

Kementerian Kewangan Malaysia. (2020). *Sukuk Prihatin Knowledge Pack*, www.maybank2u.com.my/iwov-resources/pdf/personal/wealth/sukuk-prihatin_knowledge-pack.pdf.

Malaysian Takaful Association. (2021). *COVID-19: Assistance and Coverage by Takaful Operators*, www.malaysiantakaful.com.my/sites/default/files/2021-06/Takaful%20Operators%20Assistance%20and%20Coverage%20for%20COVID-19%20%28May%202021%29%20-additional%20benefit%20as%20at%20May%202021_0.pdf.

Manzor, Z. (2021). *Skim mySalam: Pesakit Covid-19 layak dapat RM50 sehari*, www.kosmo.com.my/2021/07/28/skim-mysalam-beri-rm50-sehari-kepada-pesakit-covid-19.

MERCY Malaysia. (2021). *Donations Received*, https://mercyfightscovid19.com.

Mohamed, H. (2020). *My Say: Financing Covid-19 Stimulus Packages with GDP-Linked Sukuk*, www.theedgemarkets.com/article/my-say-financing-covid19-stimulus-packages-gdplinked-sukuk.

Mohamed, H. and Mobin, M. A. (2020). Debt Forgiveness and Debt Relief for Covid-19 Economic Recovery Financed through GDP-Linked Sukuk. *European Journal of Islamic Finance*, **16**, doi: https://doi.org/10.13135/2421-2172/4582.

Nada, G. (2020). *The COVID-19 Blow to Iran's Economy*, https://iranprimer.usip.org/blog/2020/apr/29/covid-19-blow-iran%E2%80%99s-economy.

National Zakat Foundation. (2021). *Impact Report and Financial Statements for the Year Ended 31 December 2021*, https://nzf.org.uk/wp-content/uploads/2021/08/NZF_Annual_Report_2020_.pdf.

New Straits Times. (2020). *Govt Rolls Out Additional RM166mil New Sukuk Prihatin Issuance*, www.nst.com.my/business/2020/09/625893/govt-rolls-out-additional-rm166mil-new-sukuk-prihatin-issuance.

Nomran, N. M. & Haron, R. (2021). The Impact of COVID-19 Pandemic on Islamic versus Conventional Stock Markets: International Evidence from Financial Markets. *Future Business Journal*, **7**(33). https://doi.org/10.1186/s43093-021-00078-5.

Nurdiana, T. (2021). Garuda Indonesia (GIAA) tunda bayar sukuk global US$ 500 juta & tunjuk penasihat baru. https://industri-kontan-co-id.translate.goog/news/garuda-indonesia-giaa-tunda-bayar-sukuk-global-us-500-juta-tunjuk-penasihat-baru?_x_tr_sl=id&_x_tr_tl=en&_x_tr_hl=en-GB&_x_tr_pto=op,sc.

Pakistan Centre for Philanthropy. (2020). *Covid-19 Emergency: Philanthropy Reaching Out to People*, https://pcp.org.pk/ELetter/E-Letter-Apr2020/index.htm.

Reksodiputro, H. (2015). Allen & Overy Advises Garuda Indonesia on Its Landmark USD500 Million Sukuk Issuance. www.allenovery.com/en-gb/global/news-and-insights/news/allen–overy-advises-garuda-indonesia-on-its-landmark-usd500-million-sukuk-issuance.

Reuters. (2012). Qatar Regulator Seeks to Extend Islamic Window Ban. www.reuters.com/article/islamic-finance-qatar-idUSL6E8LB01R20121011.

Samuelson, P. A. (1976). *Economics*, New York: McGraw-Hill.

Securities Commission Malaysia. (2020). Resolutions of the Shariah Advisory Council of the Securities Commission Malaysia. www.sc.com.my/api/documentms/download.ashx?id=5f0c31dc-daa9-43c1-80ac-e7ecf70c8e44.

Sherif, M. (2020). The Impact of Coronavirus (COVID-19) Outbreak on Faith-Based Investments: An Original Analysis. *Journal of Behavioral and Experimental Finance*, **28**: 100403. doi: 10.1016/j.jbef.2020.100403.

Solé, J. (2017). Introducing Islamic Banks into Conventional Banking Systems. IMF Working Paper. www.imf.org/external/pubs/ft/wp/2007/wp07175.pdf.

Sunan Ibn Majah. (n.d.). *The Book of the Sunnah*, https://sunnah.com/ibnmajah: 242.

Takaful Brunei. (2020). *Over 200 Bottles of Disinfectants Donated*, https://takafulbrunei.com.bn/news/over-200-bottles-of-disinfectants-donated.

Tehran Stock Exchange. (2020A). *Investors Record Highest Participation in IPO*, www.tse.ir/en/news/newsPages/news_N55620.html.

Tehran Stock Exchange. (2020B). *The First Virtually-Conducted IPO at TSE*, www.tse.ir/en/news/newsPages/news_N55746.html.

Tehran Stock Exchange. (2020C). *Tehran Stock Exchange Holds Largest IPO of Its History*, www.tse.ir/en/news/newsPages/news_N56022.html.

Tehran Stock Exchange. (2020D). *A New Cement Company Joins Tehran Stock Market*, www.tse.ir/en/news/newsPages/news_N56604.html.

Tehran Stock Exchange. (2020E). *A Virtual IPO: Parsian Leasing Co. joins Tehran Stock Exchange*, www.tse.ir/en/news/newsPages/news_N56664.html.

Tehran Stock Exchange. (2020F). *Abadan Power Generation Company Joins Tehran Stock Market*, www.tse.ir/en/news/newsPages/news_N56773.html.

Tehran Stock Exchange. (2020G). *The Largest Iranian Pasta Exporter Listed on TSE*, www.tse.ir/en/news/newsPages/news_N56813.html.

Tehran Stock Exchange. (2020H). *Iran's Major Investment Bank Floated Shares in Tehran Stock Exchange*, www.tse.ir/en/news/newsPages/news_N56868.html.

Tehran Stock Exchange. (2020I). *Construction Company Floats Equities on TSE*, www.tse.ir/en/news/newsPages/news_N56926.html.

Tehran Stock Exchange. (2020J). *Millions Own a Construction Co. in Tehran's Bourse*, www.tse.ir/en/news/newsPages/news_N57158.html.

Tehran Stock Exchange. (2020K). *A New IPO: Bouali Sina Petrochemical Company Joins TSE*, www.tse.ir/en/news/newsPages/news_N59808.html.

Tehran Stock Exchange. (2021A). *TSE Hosts New Mining Processing Company*, www.tse.ir/en/news/newsPages/news_N63258.html.

Tehran Stock Exchange. (2021B). *TSE Hosts New Issuer in Food Industry*, www.tse.ir/en/news/newsPages/news_N67819.html.

Tehran Stock Exchange. (2021C). *New Leasing Issuer Floats on TSE*, www.tse.ir/en/news/newsPages/news_N67924.html.

Tehran Stock Exchange. (2021D). *The Financial Holding of Civil Servants Pension Fund Went Public on TSE*, www.tse.ir/en/news/newsPages/news_N67980.html.

Tehran Stock Exchange. (2021E). *The Broiler Integration Listed on TSE*, www.tse.ir/en/news/newsPages/news_N68216.html.

The Scoop. (2021). *Takaful Brunei Keluarga Provides Free COVID-19 Coverage*, https://thescoop.co/2021/09/23/takaful-brunei-keluarga-provides-free-covid-19-coverage.

The Star. (2021). *Airline Garuda Indonesia Defaults on US$500mil Sukuk*, www.thestar.com.my/aseanplus/aseanplus-news/2021/06/19/airline-garuda-indonesia-defaults-on-us500mil-sukuk.

The Sun Daily. (2021). *Banks Collaborating with AKPK to Assist B50 Borrowers through Urus*, www.thesundaily.my/business/banks-collaborating-with-akpk-to-assist-b50-borrowers-through-urus-EF8465666.

United Nations High Commissioner for Refugees (UNHCR). (2021). *Zakat House of Kuwait*, https://giving.unhcr.org/voices/en/partner/zakat-house-of-kuwait.

Utusan Malaysia. (2020). *Lanjutan moratarium beri manfaat 262,000 Sahabat AIM*, www.utusan.com.my/berita/2020/11/lanjutan-moratarium-beri-manfaat-262000-sahabat-aim.

Wakaf Muamalat. (2020). *Wakaf Updates*, www.muamalat.com.my/wakafmuamalat/Berita-Wakaf/2020/sumbangan-wakaf-selangor-muamalat-untuk-membendung-pandemik-covid-19.html.

Wakaf Muamalat. (2021). *Wakaf Updates*, www.muamalat.com.my/wakafmuamalat/Berita-Wakaf/2021/wakaf-negeri-sembilan-muamalat-menyumbang-peralatan-kesihatan-kepada-jabatan-kesihatan-negeri-sembilan.html.

World Zakat Forum & Badan Amil Zakat Nasional (BAZNAS). (2020). *Zakat in Time of Covid-19 Pandemic: Evidence from World Zakat Forum*. Jakarta: Center of Strategic Studies – The National Board of Zakat (Puskas BAZNAS).

Widadio, N. A. (2019). *World Zakat Forum: Optimizing Funds to Reduce Poverty*, www.aa.com.tr/en/middle-east/world-zakat-forum-optimizing-funds-to-reduce-poverty/1640107.

Winosa, Y. (2020). *Indonesia's Pandemic Retail Cash Waqf-Linked Sukuk*, www.salaamgateway.com/story/indonesia-issues-pandemic-retail-cash-waqf-linked-sukuk.

Yarovaya, L., Elsayed, A., & Hammoudeh, S. (2020). *Searching for Safe Havens during the COVID-19 Pandemic: Determinants of Spillovers between Islamic and Conventional Financial Markets*, https://ssrn.com/abstract=3634114.

Ziya, M. H. & Vatanka, A. (2020). *The Iranian Government's Risky Stock Market Bet*, www.mei.edu/publications/iranian-governments-risky-stock-market-bet.

Economics of Emerging Markets

Bruno S. Sergi

Harvard University

Editor Bruno S. Sergi is an Instructor at Harvard University, and an Associate of the Harvard University Davis Center for Russian and Eurasian Studies and Harvard Ukrainian Research Institute. He is the Academic Series Editor of the Cambridge *Elements in the Economics of Emerging Markets* (Cambridge University Press), a co-editor of the *Lab for Entrepreneurship and Development* book series, and associate editor of *The American Economist*. Concurrently, he teaches International Economics at the University of Messina, is Scientific Director of the Lab for Entrepreneurship and Development (LEAD), and a co-founder and Scientific Director of the International Center for Emerging Markets Research at RUDN University in Moscow. He has published over 150 articles in professional journals and twenty-one books as author, co-author, editor, and co-editor.

About the Series

The aim of this Elements series is to deliver state-of-the-art, comprehensive coverage of the knowledge developed to date, including the dynamics and prospects of these economies, focusing on emerging markets' economics, finance, banking, technology advances, trade, demographic challenges, and their economic relations with the rest of the world, as well as the causal factors and limits of economic policy in these markets.

Cambridge Elements ☰

Economics of Emerging Markets

Elements in the Series

Printed in the United States
by Baker & Taylor Publisher Services